Negotiating Change

'This book is a rich reflection on harm principles in corporate ethics and corporate cultures. It will be invaluable to those concerned to increase the integrity of corporate conduct.'

Professor John Braithwaite, *School of Regulation and Global Governance (RegNet), Australian National University*

Behaviour change programs fail more often than they succeed. Failure is avoidable, but not if we keep attempting change the same way.

Negotiating Change is the culmination of decades of work with global corporations in ethics, communications, behaviour change and regulatory and social compliance. The book provides a text for corporate leaders, their advisors and academics and students from several disciplines to explain why the current approach to behaviour change and compliance fails, and documents why the author's approach has been successful in more than 60 countries. The book synthesises research insights from evolutionary psychology, behavioural sciences, neuroscience and neurochemistry into a practical guide. It explains why systems for behavioural guidance and control based on beliefs, religions, ethics, cultures and the law are ineffective in our globalised, hyper-connected, multi-cultural world.

The author proposes that harm, first introduced by Hippocrates to guide the practice of medicine, provides a more useful linguistic model to engage. Harm and the Harm Principles provide an objective, independent and universal measure for assessing behaviour, applying equally regardless of race, religion, gender, age or status. Harm is culturally neutral and operates independently of laws, philosophies or codes of conduct. Harm transcends geography and time. Corporations are particularly vulnerable as they operate not just across jurisdictions and cultures, but their behaviour is influenced by the very nature of incorporation, corporate structure and stock-market pressure.

Negotiating Change contains tools for boards and senior executives who want to build a more trustworthy organisation. It will not stop bad people doing bad things, but at least the self-righteous mask of legality will be removed.

Mike Lotzof specialises in organisational change leadership and communications. His programmes have assisted corporations in more than 60 countries to become more resilient and reduce risk by strengthening their culture and improving interpersonal and organisational communications. The largest single programme involved 16,000 managers and 110,000 staff in 53 countries and 22 languages.

Negotiating Change

Overcoming Entrenched Harmful
Behaviours and Beliefs

Mike Lotzof

LONDON AND NEW YORK

First published 2019
by Routledge
2 Park Square, Milton Park, Abingdon, Oxon OX14 4RN

and by Routledge
711 Third Avenue, New York, NY 10017

Routledge is an imprint of the Taylor & Francis Group, an informa business

© 2019 Mike Lotzof

The right of Mike Lotzof to be identified as author of this work has been asserted by him in accordance with sections 77 and 78 of the Copyright, Designs and Patents Act 1988.

All rights reserved. No part of this book may be reprinted or reproduced or utilised in any form or by any electronic, mechanical, or other means, now known or hereafter invented, including photocopying and recording, or in any information storage or retrieval system, without permission in writing from the publishers.

Trademark notice: Product or corporate names may be trademarks or registered trademarks, and are used only for identification and explanation without intent to infringe.

British Library Cataloguing-in-Publication Data
A catalogue record for this book is available from the British Library

Library of Congress Cataloging-in-Publication Data
Names: Lotzof, Mike, author.
Title: Negotiating change : overcoming entrenched harmful behaviours and beliefs / Mike Lotzof.
Description: Abingdon, Oxon ; New York, NY : Routledge, 2019. |
Includes bibliographical references and index.
Identifiers: LCCN 2018022024| ISBN 9780815363583 (hardback) |
ISBN 9780815363606 (pbk.) | ISBN 9781351108799 (ebook)
Subjects: LCSH: Organizational change. | Organizational behavior. |
Leadership.
Classification: LCC HD58.8 .L68 2019 | DDC 658.4/06–dc23
LC record available at https://lccn.loc.gov/2018022024

ISBN: 978-0-8153-6358-3 (hbk)
ISBN: 978-0-8153-6360-6 (pbk)
ISBN: 978-1-351-10879-9 (ebk)

Typeset in Times New Roman
by Integra Software Services Pvt. Ltd.

Contents

About the author	vii
Preface: Our global dilemma	viii
Acknowledgements	xiii

PART I
The human animal   **1**

1	How our primitive DNA shapes moral behaviour	3
2	How beliefs, religion, ethics and the law shape behaviour	23
3	The nature of trust	55

PART II
Harm   **69**

4	Harms	71
5	The harm principles	82

PART III
Harm and the corporation   **107**

6	Drivers of corporate behaviour	109
7	The role of corporate values	126
8	Culture is critical	135

vi *Contents*

9 The value of 'do no harm' in changing your organisation   146

10 The harms inherent in business   153

Index   167

About the author

Mike Lotzof specialises in organisational change leadership and communications. His programmes have assisted corporations in more than 60 countries become more resilient and reduce risk by strengthening their culture and improving interpersonal and organisational communications. The largest single programme involved 16,000 managers and 110,000 staff in 53 countries and 22 languages.

Mike has augmented his formal training in law, philosophy, psychology and economics at the University of Sydney, with the intensive study of advances in neurolinguistics, neuroscience and inherited behaviour. As a senior executive in mega and small corporations, Mike was responsible for changing and growing organisations from the inside. For the past decade he has been a trusted adviser to Boards and senior executives.

Mike is currently documenting the successful communication and change models and strategies he has refined through his extensive and varied career. He is also developing material for children to assist them become more effective communicators.

Mike lives in the South of France with his wife and two dogs.

Also by Mike Lotzof:

- *Insights to Genius – lessons in innovation and leadership*
- *2 Minute Guide to Compliance Ethics Governance and Risk*
- *Australian Insolvency Practitioners' Code of Practice*
- *The Case of Green Ham*
- *The Case of the Disappearing Ducks*
- *No Short Cuts* (screenplay)
- *Dream Runners* (screenplay)

Preface
Our global dilemma

We live in an interconnected world, seamlessly communicating, travelling and conducting business across national and cultural boundaries, and we do this with no shared understanding of what is right or wrong, good or evil. The lack of shared meaning makes it impossible to communicate effectively: to form opinions and make judgements about what is acceptable and unacceptable behaviour. Without a common understanding, it is hard, if not impossible, to resolve issues and to achieve reconciliation and a degree of harmony.

This lack of understanding of how we communicate, perceive meaning and discern right from wrong is at the heart of why the overwhelming preponderance of corporate behaviour change programmes fail. To build and implement an effective change programme requires us to truly understand our behavioural evolution. Logic, data and fact were not how we organised and behaved. These are relatively recent constructs which we use to suppress our core innate drivers. We place logic and reason on a pedestal, denying our innate 'animal' drivers and biological systems that unconsciously influence how we feel, perceive and react.

Enforced change, no matter how beneficial, triggers responses in our 'animal' brain and chemical and nervous systems. When change threatens our security, or our beliefs, the innate response overwhelms logic, data and facts. Truth becomes meaningless. Most corporate change programs embody threats to our job security and our belief about how things should be done.

Negotiating Change addresses the non-logical, animal barriers to change which is critical, particularly when a change program involves shifts in values and entrenched beliefs to change behaviours. In this situation the problem is magnified, requiring the application of the Harm Principles.

For millennia, mankind existed in relatively homogenous, semi-isolated tribes and communities. The isolation made possible the development and application of accepted local codes of behaviour, often founded on religious belief, with strong moral imperatives and taboos. What was right and wrong was clear. The standards and laws were understood.

Differences in the codes observed in neighbouring tribes and villages became apparent on the rare occasions they encountered each other and when they did, the interaction was often violent.

Preface ix

The physical isolation has disappeared in the equivalent of a biological and sociological evolutionary eye-blink. Technology-enhanced globalisation is destroying the last vestiges of separation, unwittingly unleashing clashes of values, principles and behaviours; generating frustration, misunderstanding and seemingly irreconcilable conflict.

Instantaneous forms of communication, once perceived as unifying technologies that would bind us together, have proven to simultaneously join and tear us apart by making differences visible and omnipresent. Technology is unlocking the power of new myths and creating instant, boundary-less virtual tribes. New apparent truths proliferate, unconstrained by fact, logic or the tempering quality of time.

The conflicts of difference in values are visible on the endless bad news media cycle, amplified by unconstrained social media commentary, where beliefs masquerade as facts and truth is irrelevant. Daily, we witness conflicts of beliefs, values and laws. Each faction clings, often violently, to the correctness and superiority of its dogma. Opponents on all sides claim the moral high ground. We are right; they are wrong. This impasse comes about because the meanings of right and wrong depend on who you are and where you are at a given point in time.

The problem exists not only in societies and nation states. Every organisation that has a multi-cultural workforce, has customers and suppliers from different countries, and, critically, has operations spanning continents, countries, cultures and legal systems, is at risk of avoidable conflict spawned by difference. Boards face a difficult, if not impossible, task to ensure their corporate values, principles and policies are implemented in every part of the organisation. But how do you get accord when there is no shared understanding of what is acceptable behaviour? How do you convey meaning that is immune from reinterpretation to fit local custom and practice?

This is not an academic exercise. Regulators are extending their reach beyond their national borders, demanding adherence to standards, often in conflict with local laws, custom and practice. The fines are in the tens of billions of dollars. Artful exploitation of legal loopholes, mixed with blatant self-interested disregard of laws, is destroying trust in corporations already damaged by the 2008 global financial crisis (GFC).

Corporations have responded defensively, instilling simplistic '*comply or die*', rule-based corporate control systems and tick-a-box mandatory training. This approach has failed to stem the tide of gross regulatory violations, and socially unacceptable behaviour. Command and control models fail to engage staff, breeding instead resentment and disengagement. Rules and regulations require compliance but foster a simultaneous search for gaps and ways to be within the letter of the law, while blatantly disregarding the spirit and intent. Critically, the language assumes a common understanding and acceptance of what the corporation declares to be right and wrong. This is patently absurd in our globalised world.

How effective can a Board-approved, centrally-imposed suite of policies, business principles and codes of conduct be when they conflict with employee core cultural beliefs and value systems?

What staff believe to be right or wrong, good or bad, may be different from that dictated by the imposed code. The conflicts are inextricably bound to the

x *Preface*

local context: country, culture, custom, religion and even moment in history. The very use of the language of right and wrong forestalls resolution of the dilemma.

We must fix this, but how?

Historically, three sources have been used to guide and judge behaviour: religions; cultural norms/customs; and laws/regulations. Philosophers have attempted to place these wellsprings into logical, often aspirational frameworks that appeal to reason, and the *special* nature of mankind. Ethicists discuss, debate and conjure up complex models to explain what could work, but in practice rarely does. These systems fail to provide a universal framework. They are flawed by their reliance on context.

In order to achieve aligned good behaviours, we need to change two things:

First, we need to recognise that simply educating someone about the 'truth' will not change behaviour. We need to tap into the inherited biological behavioural drivers that operate independently of the superior, data and logic based, cognitive power of human beings.

Second, we need to have a common understanding of what constitutes good behaviour. To do this we need a universal metric and language that is independent of religious, cultural, legal or individual difference.

The approach proposed in *Negotiating Change*, is to abandon the language of judgement founded in religion, culture, philosophy and law, replacing it with the neutral language of harm. Harm is a universal, culturally independent and readily understandable foundation for guiding behaviour.

The impact of harms is the same, regardless of colour, creed, sex, age, sexual orientation, class, nationality or geography. Harm is a constant that operates independently of religions, philosophies, customs or laws and even transcends time. Harm is unique, in both its universality of application and critically, in how it appeals to our visceral animal brain.

The value of the language of harm has been proven in workshops conducted in more than 60 countries. Tens of thousands of senior management and staff instantly grasped the idea of harm and applied harm theory directly to their actions and responsibilities, both in their personal life and within their organisation. They identified harmful and potentially harmful business behaviours without needing to refer to impenetrable tomes of policies and procedures, resorting to acrimonious debates or having to make value judgements of what was right or wrong, or acceptable practice. They could clearly see the harms, even if the harmful actions were permitted by law, custom or their corporate policy.

Using harm to assess corporate and individual behaviour had a profound impact. Attendees rapidly deduced that harmful behaviours were regularly justified on the basis that the actions were legal and/or culturally acceptable. The defences of '*It was legal. I operated within the law following legal advice*', and, '*It is the way things are done here*', were exposed for what they were: a justification for harmful behaviour in pursuit of profit and bonuses. These insights were achieved without any reference to values, codes of conduct or some moral testament. The Harm Principles were sufficient in themselves. The result was raised consciousness and a deep resonance that would potentially impact future

Preface xi

decision-making and behaviour. Staff felt good when they recognised that what they were doing was harm free. They felt bad when they identified the harms inherent in their work: the perfect fusion of the animal and logical, eliminating individual and collective barriers to changing behaviour.

The primary goal of *Negotiating Change* is to provide a tool for corporations to improve behaviour. The linguistics of harm provides a more robust, globally relevant basis for shaping corporate culture, regardless of industry, size or structure. Harm can easily be embedded in corporate values and codes of conduct, or used to add meaning and more deeply embed what is required. Harm can even be included in decision matrices alongside risk assessment.

The questions and decisions change from 'Is it legal?' to

'Even if it is legal, is it harmful?'

The value to corporations of using the language of harm is substantial.

1. Preventing harm reduces costs of managing regulatory intervention, the financial liability to pay fines and to reimburse customers.
2. Removing the fear of harm builds trustworthiness. Being trusted is a critical business enabler.
3. Harm is relevant and resonates with all employees at all levels, in all locations across the globe, building alignment of purpose and engagement.

In isolation, the Harm Principles will not change corporate behaviour. Inevitably, avoiding harm will set up conflicts with the pursuit of short-term profits, recognition, reward and the exercise of power. On the positive side, there is a growing understanding of the link between customer loyalty, profit, growth and being trusted. This is driving smart corporations to actively pursue trustworthiness. A corporate mindset of not doing harm will build trust, both internally with staff at all levels across the organisation, increasing engagement, and externally with customers, suppliers, the community and regulators.

At a minimum, the analysis of the potential harm of a proposed course of action will strip away the veil many corporate decision makers hide behind. They will no longer be able to disguise their decisions with conveniently opaque language and legally and culturally nuanced interpretations of right and wrong. Decision makers will know they deliberately decided to inflict harm.

The Harm Principles apply equally to the world beyond corporations. The Harm Principles do not conflict with most of the broader behavioural principles espoused in religions, philosophies, laws and enumerated human rights. Each of these wellspring systems can be deconstructed and reframed using the language of harm. The faithful can integrate harm into their thinking without denying their faith. Libertarians, utilitarians and humanists can align their models to harm. As with corporate decision makers, the faithful may still choose to inflict righteous harm in pursuit of their faith, but at least the harm they inflict will be perpetrated consciously.

xii *Preface*

Harm is a linguistic Rosetta Stone for describing and analysing behaviour in a way that has meaning and relevance to every individual.

*****

Negotiating Change is divided into three parts.

Part I The human animal, examines the broad drivers of human behaviour:

1. How our primitive DNA shapes moral behaviour
2. How beliefs, religion, ethics and the law shape behaviour
3. The nature of trust

Part II Harm defines what is and is not a harm and provides a model for applying harm to real world evaluation of conduct.

4. Harms
5. The harm principles

Part III Harm and the corporation, examines the corporate world and the application of harm inside the corporation.

6. The drivers of corporate behaviour
7. The role of corporate values in shaping employee behaviour
8. Culture is critical
9. The value of 'do no harm' to your organisation
10. Harms in business

Initially, I had included a wide-reaching discussion on harm in society which explored the application of the harm principles to a selected number of current social issues such as the origin and limits of human rights and the war on drugs, but was persuaded to publish them separately as a companion for those interested in the broader applications of harm theory.

A third publication, *How?* planned for publication in 2019, will codify all the practices refined in decades of workshops in more than 60 countries. The goal: to increase the effectiveness of communications and change programmes, regardless of the subject matter.

It is assumed throughout this book that the guiding minds of organisations want their organisations to be trustworthy, well-behaved and sustainable. For time-poor business leaders, I have kept the text to a minimum, editing down case-studies and examples which will be progressively published on-line in easy to digest PowerPoint packages.

For the philosophers, ethicists, jurists and legislators, I hope the ideas stimulate debate and a more rigorous analysis of the role of harm in broader society and in shaping laws, regulation and regulatory practices.

For those with malevolent intent, as my children say – not so much!

Acknowledgements

I am indebted to two towering figures in the world of regulation and corporate behaviour: Professor Malcolm Sparrow of the Kennedy School of Government, Harvard University, who introduced me to the concept of harm and Professor John Braithwaite, founder of REGNET at the Australian National University, whose ideas tempered and informed my thinking and whose questions and passion for making the world a better place ensured that Principle 6 was included.

Much of my understanding of communications and influence is derived from endless discussions with my long-time friend and mentor, Allan Parker.

The ideas in this book have been a lifetime in gestation, from my unsuccessful quest as an undergraduate in search of the 'ultimate ethic', to animated discussions with associates and clients around the world. The ideas could not have been shaped and refined without the constructive input, criticism and debate with my colleagues and friends Heather, Pascal and Ali and feedback from the hundreds of change leaders in more than 50 countries, who placed their trust in me, successfully implementing my theories with their bosses and colleagues.

This book would never have been finished without the enduring support and encouragement of my wife, Caren.

*****

I like to imagine Hippocrates pondering his first principle:

> *If in doubt, first, do no harm*

He is shaking his head, wondering why an idea that is so simple and elegant is so poorly applied in our modern world.

As you read this book, I would like you to keep in the back of your mind a marvellous insight that I have respectfully adapted:

> *The only thing necessary for harm to triumph,*
> *is for good men and women to do nothing.*

Part I
The human animal

1 How our primitive DNA shapes moral behaviour

Key points:

- Survival of our primitive ancestors improved when they exhibited behaviours such as fear and distrust of others, belonging to a tribe, following leaders, trusting members of their own tribe and reciprocal altruism.
- Those that survived passed on survival-enabling characteristics. The resulting behaviours were genetically 'hard-wired' and operated automatically.
- The evolution of human high level cognitive function did not replace the automatic survival system.
- Logic, reason, data and facts are the building blocks of our cognitive function. By contrast, hard wiring of behaviours and the associated chemical triggers drive the primitive survival.

Conclusion

- Our superior cognitive ability masks the operation of our inherited behavioural drivers.
- Taming our primitive DNA is critical to building a civil society.

For the corporation

- Changing staff behaviour requires the simultaneous addressing of both the cognitive rational functions AND the primitive automatic drivers.
- The failure of corporate ethics, compliance and change programmes has its roots in the over-reliance on the cognitive domain.

4 *The human animal*

Human biological evolution has been relatively stagnant for millennia. Our core being; our primitive fear, fight, flight, trust and distrust biological survival mechanisms have not evolved. They have failed to adapt to the social evolution from nomadic hunter-gatherer families; to tribes; tribes to villages; villages to cities; and the amalgamation of physical cities into the relatively modern invention of nation states. We are now being drawn inexorably into the sputtering emergence of the global village, driven by population growth, mass migration and the exponential growth in knowledge, communications technology and globalised commerce.

We use our rational cognitive ability and stored knowledge to try to appreciate what these tectonic forces presage for how we should act and organise. Unfortunately, our cognitive, technical, cultural and social evolution have outstripped our inherited survival biology. The analytic models we use to found and guide our social institutions and then to discuss and understand these changes are primarily rational and logical. Even our innermost thoughts are couched in unspoken words that whisper in our inner ear like Iago, counselling, prodding, suggesting, but always conscious.

But our automatic systems operate silently. They are the engine of gut feel; how we know without knowing why; how we feel without being able to 'put our finger on it'. It is the intangible drivers that confound our logical, rational approach at organising personal and collective behaviour. Our superbly rational cognitive powers are doomed to failure if we ignore our primitive drivers.

Our attempts at rational analysis often conflict with and mask the powerful underlying primitive biological survival mechanisms that were essential to our club-wielding hunter-gatherer ancestors, but are, more often than not, an impediment to internet-enabled, multi-cultural, modern business warriors. Our ability to think, reason, amass and access a vast fund of knowledge disguises why we so often behave as we do – emotionally, illogically and irrationally. Logic and reasoning are incapable of completely overriding our inherent primitive behaviour mechanisms and drivers.

Understanding these underlying non-logical drivers of behaviour is essential if we want to change mindset and future behaviour. The lack of understanding of the biology of behaviour is one of the root causes for the failure of social and corporate change programmes. Tabloid politicians and warlords understand and exploit these drivers. They appeal to primitive nativism, which is essentially illogical but explains why good men do bad things.

Globalising forces wreak havoc with our biology. Our primal being seeks comfort in the safety and similarity of tribal islands, while globalisation forces us to confront diversity and difference. We are required to be politically correct in how we think and act in every field of our operation. We are called on to be citizens of the world, embracing multiculturalism, but this assumes we are logical beings, who can divorce our thoughts from our feelings.

We do not yet understand the full nature of brain chemistry and how it drives behaviours. The role of cortisol production during times of stress in preparing us for fight or flight; our urge to reproduce; to gain power; to dominate; to overindulge our pleasure senses; is the stuff of tabloids and pulp fiction. What the tabloids fail to tell us is that cortisol also inhibits rational/logical cerebral functions. We operate by instinct. 'My DNA made me', is only part of the picture. Cortisol is the most popularised brain chemical, but it is only one of many. It is only the tip of the biological behavioural iceberg.

What follows is a very brief introduction into a controversial and emerging science. It is set out in the first chapter, not because inherited biological mechanisms are the most important drivers of behaviour, but because they are often ignored in our quest to place ourselves on a cognitive pedestal – superior, uniquely rational, ethical animals. Aloft on our pedestal, we are asserting that we are not primitive animals driven by biology. We are fooling ourselves. The impact of innate drivers will be used in the following chapters to partly explain why our cognitive approach to behaviour change fails.

1.1 The survival imperative

The Survival Imperative is the base underlying behavioural assumption. It overrides all our other drivers when we believe we are in danger. Our ancestors, as with all life, were programmed to maximise the survival of their DNA through procreation. Those best adapted to survive, and thus procreate, passed on their DNA, which included drivers that enhanced survival. Survival, however, was not just about strength, speed and intelligence. Alongside those attributes were mechanisms that drove fear, belonging, trusting and the willingness to follow. The brain chemistry and inherited automatic behaviours that aided survival proliferated, encoded in DNA.

1.2 Fear and distrust of difference

Effective danger recognition plus fight or flight responses increased the chance of survival, and thus the ability to reproduce and pass on the supporting genetic fear mechanism. Fear is a response to danger, real, perceived or imagined. Fear sometimes manifests as extreme phobias – spiders, snakes, deep water and radiation. Fear is not always rational, but to the fearful it is very real. This fear mechanism persists today, residing in the primitive sectors of the brain, over which we have limited conscious control.

One of our primitive fears was to fear others. For our ancestors 'others' would have been people from a different clan, or tribe, who in the absence of trade were more likely to be motivated to steal your stores, capture your women and kill the male opposition than to invite you in for a drink, or share a haunch of mammoth. The fear, or distrust of difference, became a genetically programmed, chemically enhanced reaction that triggers us to mistrust or fear 'others'. It is a biological, non-rational response to danger – real or imagined.

Today, when visibly different people enter 'our' space, there is an automatic response, defensive or aggressive. It is the animal order. Philosophers and ethicists do not like to admit that our superior consciousness can be subordinated

6   *The human animal*

to primitive, automatic impulses. Nor do we like to diminish the image of ourselves as cerebral, logical, superior and, for some, divinely created beings.

Unfortunately, the reality is that fear is one of the most powerful forces that cannot easily be overcome through logic and learning. It requires a programme of exposure and desensitisation, actual experience, that mutes the automatic brain chemistry response. It is the process of habituation, a process that was illustrated to biology students who watched a humble snail grow confident and come out of its shell when the danger signal (that of the students tapping on its shell or whatever the signal was) failed to cause it harm.

The fear induced by racial difference is well-documented. Yet even the most fearful can, with sufficient contact and exposure, lose their fear/flight response. Condemning fear of others as racist, xenophobic or extremist is a denial of our DNA. Tolerance, acceptance and compassion to others is not part of our inherited biology. Tolerance is inculcated. It must be embedded emotionally, not just learnt as an abstract, politically correct rule. An example of this is the wave of migrants generating fear in many communities across Western Europe. Unsurprisingly, those in the front line, in the Greek and Italian islands to which the migrants headed, have the most exposure to the plight of the migrating individuals. They show compassion once they have become habituated to the 'others'. When the amorphous, fear-inducing 'others' take shape, have names, smile and cry, although different, they become more like us.

By contrast, those who only deal with a depersonalised abstract 'other' continue to react negatively – even violently. This is natural, but in our globalised politically correct world, it is unacceptable. Irrational xenophobia has a biological root cause that cannot be changed by telling or simplistic education, dictate or rule of law.

1.3   Belonging to tribes

While fear of others was one force, primitive man increased security by belonging to a group – a family, a clan, a tribe. Belonging to tribes supported individual survival. Belonging enhanced safety and reduced fear – real and perceived. Those who were happy to belong survived, passing on the 'belonging' gene. The need to belong drove the evolution of tribes into societies. As societies grew they developed operating rules to manage increasing complexity.

Tribalism and belonging are alive and well, finding modern expression in teams, sports-fans, social groups, villages, cities and national identities. For the religious, there is not just comfort in support from the chosen God, but also from belonging to a religious infrastructure with fellow believers. Armed forces and wars are built on the exploitation of belonging. The military invests considerable effort in building identity with country, flag, service, down to the smallest operating unit.

Belonging provides not only safety but can also provide a central element of individual identity. It appears that we were not programmed to have a single identity. We can align ourselves to family, tribe, macro-tribes such as nations, religions or even political systems and sports teams. Each tribe to which we belong has its own code and demands for loyalty.

The same is true in corporations. With the right mix of leadership, environment and purpose we build identity, a sense of belonging and loyalty to the company we work for. This need to belong is exploited by leaders and marketers. It makes us vulnerable and is a biological root cause of many poor behaviours.

1.4 Trusting

> For it is mutual trust, even more than mutual interest that holds human associations together. Our friends seldom profit us but they make us feel safe.
>
> (HL Menken)

The biological survival imperative discussed earlier suggests that we all start from a position of fear – of mistrust. But mistrust alone was not sufficient for our primitive ancestors to survive. To thrive and survive they needed the support of others. They belonged to tribes and in the act of belonging they necessarily trusted their tribe to keep them safe. Belonging requires a mechanism for trusting in the group, for trusting individuals within the group and, in particular, trusting the group's leader. The ultimate role of leaders is to make followers feel safe.

Survival dictated the need to simultaneously trust 'us' and distrust 'others'.

The trust mechanism operates differently to that of fear. Fear is involuntary and instantaneous. Trust, by contrast, is built over time, usually with some experiential or empirical basis. Trust can be built on fact, personal experience or the experience and opinions of others in whom we have placed trust. Ultimately, trust is a belief, built in part on rational grounds.

Trust has two primary dimensions. The act of trusting and the state of being trustworthy. Both are important and can operate independently.

A fool can trust without any basis. The trust may be misplaced in someone who is not trustworthy. Conversely, a person may be trustworthy, but not trusted for unrelated factors such as race, religion, age, gender or context.

Trustworthiness is not unique to human interaction. While we often talk about people being trustworthy, the concept can be applied equally to a vast range of animate and inanimate objects and natural phenomena. My car is reliable. I trust it will get me where I need to go. I trust this brand. I have used it for years. I trust my dog.

Trust is not binary. There is a scale. A simple example illustrates both the source of trusting and the degree to which something is trusted.

- I do not trust this bridge. It looks unsafe.
- I have no idea whether or not to trust this bridge.
- I am not sure if I trust this bridge. A stranger said he crossed it yesterday, but he is half my weight and he looked shifty.

8   *The human animal*

- I think I trust this bridge, because Bill, whom I trust because he has never ever let me down and I have known him a long time, said he crossed it this morning and Bill is heavier than me.
- I trust this bridge because I just watched Bill walk across it and he is heavier than me.
- I trust this bridge because I was the builder and know how it was constructed.

In each of the above there is a mixture of empirical, experiential and emotional reasons for the degree of trust. There is also a special category of trusting: blind trust – leaps of faith, such as the religious approach, which requires no empirical support.

- I don't worry, because I trust, that if the bridge collapses, God will save me.

1.5 The interaction of fear and trust

If I start from a position of morbid fear, say being scared of heights, no amount of reasoning would be sufficient to assuage my fear of the bridge. I would stand transfixed on one side. However, if crossing the bridge was the only route to escape imminent death, I might need no convincing at all and simply allow the greater fear to overwhelm the lesser lack of trust.

When our biology of fear kicks in, it makes it difficult to trust, for example, big dogs with loud barks and sharp teeth. Our trust may increase, and fear decrease, if the dog is on a leash held by its owner and we know and trust the owner. If we have interacted with the dog many times without incident, we may start to trust it, but still be a little fearful, a sign that there is latent distrust. In cultures where dogs are rarely kept as household pets, even small, cute, harmless dogs elicit high levels of irrational distrust, anxiety and even fear.

The push-pull of fear and trust is important. Fear is instant. Building trust takes time. Trust building takes place when people are:

- Reliable;
- Consistent;
- Predictable;
- Truthful;
- Honest; and
- Loyal.

Being trusted on one dimension does not implicitly make you trustworthy on another.

- I trust Bill to be here on time, but not to do the accounts.
- The car always starts but is unstable at speeds over 60.

Each of these and the myriad other dimensions requires judgement from the person giving the trust. To make an informed judgement, rather than simply guessing, or having faith, requires some form of empirical evidence. In all these examples, trustworthiness is earned over time because of a consistency of behaviours.

First-hand experience is a primary generator of trust, though not necessarily the most accurate. Most scams are fabricated by first building trust in one dimension to then exploit a weakness in another.

Trust is a perception. It may be factual but equally it may be a fantasy. Even when it is a fantasy, the impact on behaviour is that once we trust, we act as if the object in which we trust is trustworthy.

An interesting characteristic of trust building (explored in more detail in Chapter 4), is the power of peer groups and leaders (actual, icon, cultural and thought) to influence in whom we trust and the degree to which we extend trust. It is the basis of political influence, gang followership, taste and popular fashion. It is the life blood of celebrity advertising and endorsement.

Our virtual, technology-enabled world is changing how we build trust. We are shifting from personal experience and reliance on trusted individuals (peers, family leaders) to trusting in the judgement and honesty of strangers. We are crowd-sourcing trust. Star ratings, likes, trending, views etc. are rapidly becoming the new trust lens, at least for purchases of goods and services. The 5-star rating of hotels can drive trade. A bad review can destroy the business.

It is astonishing that we are suspending our natural fear of others and relying on strangers. We are allowing our virtual tribe to inform our decisions. We trust them, even when the risks are substantial, such as renting a room in our home to strangers. The credibility of reviews and ratings takes on a special importance given the consequences of fabricated false and misleading reviews. I will not book this hotel because, while it has great rating scores, I don't trust the site to verify that the ratings are independent. I will book this hotel because its ratings were from real visitors.

1.6 Trust and values

Trust is independent of values. Trust is not built on the particular values that an individual has, but a belief that the values are shared and the shared values will be consistently adhered to. For example, the values held by members of gangs, church congregations and terrorist groups differ dramatically. Internally within each group the values are shared. The belief that the shared values will be abided by provides a foundation for trust within each group, between group members. In the three wildly divergent groups listed at the start of the previous section, the values held by each group are in conflict with the other groups. As a consequence, trust between the groups is almost impossible.

When we say, 'I trust A because of his values', what we are really saying is 'I trust A because he adheres to values like mine'.

10   *The human animal*

Breaching shared values generates a range of responses: disbelief, anger, fear, repulsion. Trust is diminished, if not totally destroyed. Often there is a demand for justice, the form of which will align with the values that were broken. The gang may administer a beating and expulsion. The church group may demand repentance, public penance and asking of forgiveness. Terrorists may simply execute the offender. For them this is logical and consistent with their values and because, for terrorists, adhering to their values is a matter of life and death.

Rebuilding trust is harder than building trust from scratch. In the new build, there is no specific fear beyond the 'normal background noise'. When rebuilding, the act of betrayal of trust creates a sub-zero starting point. The negative residue is an empirically quantifiable fear that recognises that what happened once may happen again, though the circumstances may change.

Fear and trust are polar opposites, but not necessarily on the same axis like trust and distrust. The relationship between distrust and fear is more complex. Not everything distrusted generates fear, but fear generates distrust. As they say – '*it's complicated*'.

1.7 The biology of trusting

While all the forgoing suggests that trustworthiness is a logical, experiential outcome, the knowledge we are building on the brain chemistry of trusting challenges that conclusion. There is a molecule, oxytocin, present in the brain, that influences the degree of trusting and thus feelings of whether someone is trustworthy. This is a different molecule from the well-documented chemicals such as dopamine that influence our sense of well-being, or cortisol that prepares us to fight or flee.

The neuroscientist, Paul Zak, conducted controlled experiments on the impact of oxytocin. He found that artificially administering oxytocin significantly distorted the results in standardised trust tests. Participants became more trusting for no logical reason. It was purely chemical.

In subsequent field trials, Zak identified that certain behaviours involving physical contact (hugging, kissing, shaking hands) and dancing, laughing and singing stimulated the production of oxytocin. Each of these behaviours is regarded as socially positive in most modern societies. What Zak discovered was a virtuous self-reinforcing biological mechanism, triggered by customary practices, that supports the growth in social cohesion which in turn promotes survival. Oxytocin-triggering behaviours that improve tribal/group trust fit perfectly with the ideas of biologically inherited survival mechanisms that shape behaviours and interactions within societies.

Trusting is critical in human interactions. Thus, understanding the role of oxytocin and how it is produced is important. It is probable that oxytocin is produced during activities such as rituals, mass rallies, shows of solidarity, chanting, singing, rally songs, sloganeering and other group activities. The beneficiaries of chemically induced trust are primarily the leader but also the

How our primitive DNA shapes moral behaviour 11

like-minded. Oxytocin production may go some way to explaining the power of personality and cults to suppress doubt and fear, replacing those feelings with abnormal levels of trust in cult leaders, fellow cult members and the organisation to which they belong.

Corporate leaders have employed team-building activities, knowing that they generate more enthusiasm and loyalty but without understanding the biological mechanisms involved. Leaders smile, shake hands and, depending on the corporate culture, encourage hugging, cheering and the use of music to 'pump' the crowd. They are the stock-in-trade of motivational speakers and evangelical churches.

There are many questions yet to be answered. How acceptable is it to manipulate trust through seemingly benign activities? If benign manipulation of oxytocin levels is acceptable, what is the rationale for not simply delivering it in the air-conditioning?

We live in an era where trust has largely been destroyed. We do not trust our politicians, our media, our corporations. We do not trust bankers to look after our interests as well as their own. We do not trust poorly understood forces such as the market, globalisation and free trade, even though we are exposed to them every day in the media.

We live in an era of fear and terror. We worry that the core pillars of our society, our individual rights and responsibilities, may be eroded as an unintended consequence of how we combat those who do not respect laws and conventions.

Rebuilding trust is perhaps the greatest global challenge facing our leaders at every level and in every society. For the leaders of corporations, the question for you is what can you do to make your staff, customers and the communities within which you operate feel that you will keep them safe – free from harm – in your interactions with them? What will you do to rebuild trustworthiness?

This is not an altruistic quest. The pivotal role of trust for corporate sustainability is explored in Chapter 4.

1.8 Neuroscience and inherited moral behaviour

The traditional approach to influencing behaviour relies on teaching rules and consequences. It is the basis on which parents instruct their children; religions inculcate their dogma; and corporations spend billions on ethics and compliance training. Yet knowledge alone may make no difference. Knowing a rule and choosing to follow it seem to be independent mechanisms.

Theoretical and empirical developments in neuroscience and moral psychology suggest that some moral behaviours are hardwired. The social psychologist Jonathan Haidt claims to have identified five moral values, or pillars, that he says are hardwired into the new-born brain. This is extremely controversial as it brings into question the unique spiritual nature of human morality and the value of ethics training as currently delivered.

12   *The human animal*

Haidt's pillars are:

- Harm/Care;
- Fairness/Reciprocity;
- In Group Loyalty;
- Respect for Authority; and
- Purity/Sanctity.

Haidt has found high correlations between scores on the pillars and the overt expressions of conservative and liberal behaviours. Haidt's theory is supported by natural history programmes that have documented all the 'human-like' pillar behaviours in animals, except the values of purity and sanctity.

Until recently, fairness and altruism[1] were regarded as purely human traits and evidence of our special nature. This has been disproved. There are now well-documented examples of reciprocal altruism in animals as diverse as bats and rodents. Reciprocal altruism – you do for me, I'll do for you – in animal behaviours supports, but does not prove, Haidt's theory of hardwiring. Hardwiring prompts the question, 'What is the benefit of these traits/behaviours?' The simplistic answer is that these 'moral like' behaviours are inherited because they support survival through their impact on the development of the social collective. Altruism is an interesting case study. If altruism is not part of the divine human spark, then what is its mechanism and why does it exist?

First, altruism is not a selfless act. We don't give and get nothing in return. So-called altruistic acts, acts of kindness and generosity, generate oxytocin and other pleasure chemicals. We feel good by doing good. Human and animal behaviour is in part driven by avoidance of pain and partly from feeling good. We eat for pleasure, not just for the calories. We drink alcohol for the buzz. We take drugs for even more buzz. We satisfy many different desires, some intellectualised such as appreciation of art, simply to feel good. Learned appreciation suggests that we can build new pleasure pathways. Those in the know can feel good; for the rest of us, the emperor is naked.

The second, and more tangible, rationale for innate altruism is as an aid to survival. Altruistic acts are important for social cohesion. They go to the very essence of the origin and sustainability of tribes. If members of the tribe were selectively allowed to starve, or denied shelter or comfort, they would not feel safe. If they had sufficient power, they would rebel to make the society fairer, less arbitrary and safer. They would promote mutuality. Unfortunately, as so often happens, the exercise of liberating power simply replaces one tyrant with another and the elevation of one group over the others. If it was simply logical and rational, game theory would deliver different results.

Doing good enhances social cohesion and the strength of the society. It makes us safer. We have less fear that we will be harmed or abandoned. The implication is that altruism, like fear, belonging and trust, is a biologically inherited behaviour. While it has been expressed in moral precepts and religious dogma,

How our primitive DNA shapes moral behaviour   13

altruism, or more accurately, reciprocal altruism, is a good thing, not because it is moral, or God mandated, but because it helps societies survive and thrive.[2]

> Selfless acts often attract accusations of hidden selfishness, suggesting they're not really altruistic at all.
>
> (Michael Regnier)[3]

1.9 The malevolent potential of inheritance

Fears, belonging, trust, non-logical inherited hardwiring and brain chemistry undoubtedly helped us survive our primitive roots, but render us vulnerable to manipulation. These innate drivers provide insight into how 'good' people get swept up and commit atrocities.

Our fear monsters are easily fed. Our need to belong can be exploited. When fear of others and tribal belonging are paired, we readily succumb to the rhetoric, vilifying and dehumanising others. If one adds to the forces Haidt's dimensions of avoiding harm, caring for one's own, loyalty to the group and allegiance to authority one can see how the positive bonding survival mechanisms have, like Janus, a side that can easily morph from positive to malevolent.

The transition from a raucous one-eyed support for a team to violence against opposing fans is common. In the real world, we witness this transition to violence and warfare at tribal, regional and global levels. 'Blood lust', the nineteenth-century expression, may have been closer to the mark than we would like to admit.

While the creation of 'others' is the stock in trade of would-be leaders and cause promoters, at a more fundamental level, we may have an innate need to find 'others', as doing so reinforces the value of belonging to the tribe.

As relatively unworldly children and teenagers we instinctively create gangs, groups, in-crowds and losers. Now we create and belong to virtual tribes. It is vital to understand the mechanisms. The more we clothe these behaviours in philosophical and ethical language, or simplify them as a reaction to the depersonalisation and isolation of the modern world, the more we deny the power of our genetics and the more we are at risk.

Online radicalisation is a recent phenomenon. It is an extreme version of virtual tribalism. It is more than just intellectual. It has an emotional appeal that goes to the very root of our biology.

1.10 Beyond biology – ideas, myths and story

The biology of survival provides insights into why we behave as we do. It provides insights into how we organise, trust, distrust, form groups, choose leaders, strive to acquire, develop and enforce behavioural norms. The biology is compelling at the level of individuals and small tribes, but it is not sufficient to explain how humans morphed from tribes to nations. Biology fails to explain

14 *The human animal*

how our ancestors could organise into very large groups of tens of thousands when communication was limited to physical presence and the leader could not be everywhere to exercise authority and control.

Visibility of the leader in the pre-technology era was limited to direct personal contact. One person could reach hundreds, perhaps thousands, yet armies of tens of thousands followed the command of Genghis Khan, roman emperors, egyptian pharoahs, caliphs and kings. The common thread in all these was not their physical presence, but the idea they embodied. An idea, like the legends of Merlin and Arthur, which could be communicated by word of mouth through story-telling.

Whether it was divinity or destiny, followers coalesced around an idea embodied in the totemic leader. People became followers, not simply because of the personal alpha powers of a leader they had never met, but because they could belong to the leader's tribe that embodied a compelling idea, wrapped in a myth and disseminated by stories.

1.11 Belonging to ideas and myths

It is perhaps the marriage of cognitive imagined ideas, with the innate need to belong, that is the ultimate motive force driving social evolution. There is no limit to our human ability to manufacture ideas with which to align and belong. However, the very act of belonging to one idea sets up boundaries that demarcate and separate us, from those who follow other ideas. They become the 'others'.

Ideas take many forms:

- Class structures with attendant rights, obligations, duties, powers and entitlements;
- Religions;
- Nation states;
- Philosophies such as egalitarianism, liberalism, utilitarianism;
- Collective organisational principles such as democracy, communism, dictatorships;
- Economic principles such as capitalism, free markets, socialism.

Ideas extend the physical order and provide bollards on which we attach our innate drivers. The Age of Reason challenged the power of the innate. Reason became a civilising force limiting the innate survival instincts. Yet the Age of Reason contrarily harnessed the power of emotion and identification with ideas. Abolitionists, for example, belonged proudly to a tribe that was doing battle with slavers.

Identity and belonging drive loyalty. Loyalty impacts behaviour, including, in the extreme, the need to conquer and subjugate. Nation states, empires and their emotional cousins, nationalism and imperialism, were until the end of World War II the largest identifiable tribal units. Empires and imperialism ultimately collapsed because of the more powerful competing forces of local tribalism expressed as ideas of national identity. The development of the concept of the United Nations has not stopped wars. Apart from the intellectual founders, for whom the United Nations had a vibrancy and reality, for most it is seen as an abstract, depersonalised group of people in suits, talking and occasionally doing something, but with limited effectiveness and negligible efficiency.

We do not seem to rally to the abstraction of a global ideal. The UN and its smaller cousin the EU have limited mythical power to bind. It is only when there is an existential threat to humanity, such as an alien invasion or an approaching killer asteroid, that 7 billion people could be bound into a single cohesive tribe. In the absence of such an existential threat, there is no sufficiently compelling idea. Landing a man on the moon was a compelling, but transient, idea, drowned in Cold War competition. Us and them. Nuclear proliferation and the idea of mutually assured destruction has not stopped proliferation. The idea of climate change is more divisive than unifying, notwithstanding potential global catastrophes.

While it is too early to tell, it is probable that the European Union is enjoying peace, not because of alignment and identity with the EU as an idea, but rather that the EU as a market has made warfare less attractive as a means of the accumulation of wealth and the preservation of power. The freedom of movement of people, capital, goods and services does little to reduce parochial labelling such as 'Made in France', or self-preserving barriers of national politics, laws, customs and the protection of industries and ways of life.

The myth of the ennobling and enriching power of the free market and its democratic cousin are perhaps the most powerful ideas of the twenty-first century. Both have spawned wars and revolutions. Millions have signed on, powered by social media which allows us to join like-minded strangers in virtual tribes to share ideas, once only disseminated by story-tellers, books and through more traditional media channels. Where what was said was once controlled by money, proprietors and governments, now there are unrestricted channels. There is a virtual tribe for everyone at the click of a button.

The power of technology-enabled virtual tribes is their ability to have strangers across the globe coalesce around ideas, projecting the virtual tribe into the real world. It is the perfect medium for preaching and conversion. Potential recruits can stay safe behind their screens, watching, joining with the relatively risk-free anonymity and safety of physical isolation, until the newly emboldened convert decides to join. We have witnessed the power of virtual tribes to mobilise, coalesce and exercise power, but have yet to see sustainable transformation brought about by virtual tribes in the absence of aligned real-world leaders and action.

Corporations must operate in this maelstrom of belonging, the free market and enabling technologies. Corporate tribalism is alive and well, whether at the global or local level or even down to functional sub-units. The human need to belong is not extinguished at the front door of the corporation. On the contrary, it is consciously exploited by corporations to build teams out of work colleagues; to foster real and faux rivalries by building identity and loyalty. Unfortunately, as

16 *The human animal*

we will see, these sub-tribes often descend into self-serving silos, to the detriment of the corporation as a whole.

Unlike our animal cousins, humans appear to be the only specie capable of creating abstract ideas and communicating them to each other. There is no limit to the range and nature of ideas. By ideas, I do not mean invention and scientific advance, but rather abstractions, philosophies and myths – stories of the unreal. The twenty-first century gave birth to hundreds of ideas and myths. Some came and went like fashion fads. Others took the form of social movements that, because of their popularity and persistence, morphed from idea to reality such as democracy, communism, capitalism and many other isms.

In his book, *Sapiens*, Yuval Harari postulates that the force that enabled mega groups was the ability to invent and communicate myths and, in particular, the myths of Gods. There is evidence of prehistoric Gods and religions. We are all too aware of the power and influence of the multiplicity of modern religions – mainstream and sect.

Gods provide the single greatest controlling idea. Whether Gods are real or not is irrelevant. What matters is that the religious structures enabled the exercise of power beyond the immediate physicality of leadership. Religions provide control mechanisms through fear and hope. They engender a belief in the need to follow the precepts and rules. Actions of men are legitimised by cloaking them in the service of the divine.

In Harari's world, anything created through the mind of man is a myth. Into this category falls every adventure story and legend. We have created nation states, money and, of course, corporations. These are fictions, invented by man, which, while they have achieved form and substance, have a meaning, power and value beyond their intrinsic nature.

Myths are propagated through story-telling, oral and written. Written language facilitated the transmission of myth. But there are many modern tribes without a written text. They have a complex mythology that dictates their interpersonal relationships; the nexus between man and nature; and the relationship of one tribe to another. Many stories are reservoirs of survival knowledge; maps to water; food sources; tribes to be avoided and those who might be friendly. Their stories dictated kinship and boundaries for marriage.

> The myths insinuated and invisibilised themselves into the culture and culture drives behaviour.
>
> (Yuval Harari)[4]

The centuries have revealed the power of myths that enabled great and terrible leaders – Kennedy, Churchill, Hitler from the last century. Before that Alexander the Great, the Caesars, Pharoahs and Kings, who coupled their worldly power to the divine. It is one thing to argue with a man. It is another to argue with a God, or God's anointed.

At first glance, it may appear that the language of myth is difficult to incorporate into the logical metrics of the corporate world. We do not like to think of the corporation, markets, legal systems, employment, stocks and bonds as myths. They are real! Really?

We give power and allegiance to political parties, football clubs and leaders. We give value to brands, companies, currencies, shares and financial instruments without needing to worry that they are mythical constructs. We suspend our disbelief, trusting that, provided we all play within the rules of the myth, everything will be fine. Surprisingly, it usually is.

The problem arises when we start believing that the algorithms in the models of our mythical systems are empowered with insight and truth. Unfortunately, the models manipulate the myth and in doing so impact our reality. The market goes up or down triggered by billions in trades triggered by factors in a model of a man-made construct that we made real. When markets rise, we feel good, conversely when they fall. How we feel impacts how we behave and interact. We are driven by a model of our myth!

How do myths become real? They do so when they are embedded in a story we choose to believe. Once we believe, anything is possible. Kennedy gave us Camelot. Stalin gave us terror, Hitler Aryan superiority, Gorbachev glasnost and rocket scientists financial models with which to manipulate markets and tell us we are better or worse off.

Steve Jobs was as much a legend as he was a man. In *Insights to Genius*, I explore how staff related to the idealised myth of Steve Jobs and how Apple is the product of story, as are Facebook, Uber and other stocks in corporations that trade beyond logical value. Apple fanatics adhere with religious fervour, which until now has not been equalled by seemingly similar but androgynous competitors.

The next big idea, provided it is wrapped in a sexy, powerful story, will catch fire.

(Mike Lotzof)[5]

1.12 The power of story

Long before writing, our ancestors communicated and presumably told stories, some of which have been preserved in cave paintings that span continents and millennia. Stories captured and transmitted the experiential DNA that aided survival. Today every culture, every tribe, no matter how remote or sophisticated, still uses story to transmit knowledge of both their real and mythical worlds.

The Australian Aborigines have a plethora of song-lines (stories) that seamlessly weave Gods, myths and legends with real-world survival data, mapping locations of water, food, poisonous springs and medicines. The Gods struggled and were victorious. Each victory point has a geographic location that aids survival in one the world's most inhospitable environments. Stories captured and transmitted data without reference to latitude and longitude, science or mathematics. There is similar rock art in Namibia, where, unfortunately, there

18 *The human animal*

are no survivors who can communicate the real meaning. Guides tell stories created by modern archaeologists, drawing parallels with other cultures. Their conclusions are undoubtedly cross-contaminated by their own stories. Yet, visitors take these interpretative stories as gospel.

The brain processes stories differently to how it manages data. We are constantly bombarded with information through our senses. The brain is constantly sifting and sorting, from the concrete to the abstract, running scenarios, comparing the data input to previous patterns and associations. This continuous process of pattern matching and discarding happens in milliseconds. It does this in real time, in the background, below the level of consciousness. It is the basis of gut-feeling. You know, but you don't know why.

Story-telling accesses processes that simply listing data cannot. Story puts data into motion. Story is the mental equivalent of a viral inoculation. It allows the data to be transmitted as part of another process. Story is a cerebral Trojan that infects the brain, in the same way as a software Trojan infects your computer.

Story is the mental equivalent of the vectors used in molecular DNA cloning. In genetic engineering a vector is a DNA molecule used as a vehicle to carry foreign genetic material into another cell, where it can be replicated and/or expressed. In cognitive processing the story carries the information to be integrated into how people think, feel and behave. As in genetic research, not all information will be expressed. It may fall on deaf ears.

From earliest childhood, children of all nationalities create fantasy worlds. They make up stories full of heroes and demons, good and bad. They face troubles and enjoy victories. It is stories about people, animals, places, fantasies and ideas that capture young imaginations.

Story-telling is unfortunately programmed out of our lives at school, where rote learning and memorisation hold centre stage. Creativity and imagination are supressed. Flights of pure fancy are shot down by a barrage of facts, notwithstanding that few children are inspired by lists of data.

The one bastion that never gives up on stories is religion. Religions of all persuasions infiltrate young minds through stories and parables into which are woven the tenets and rules. There are other norming forces in religious practice, but the common vector is story.

Stories move teenagers and adults. Heroes and heroines, villains, good, evil, hope, despair, fiction, non-fiction, adventure, romance, morals, parables and fables are the stuff of stories and, while we suspend our disbelief, we live vicariously, atavistic, opening ourselves unwittingly to learn and change. Not all stories are designed to inform and change, but they do transmit messages. Every story has a rhythm. There is a hero. A villain. Trouble, struggle and an outcome. Along the way as we become immersed, we absorb the lessons of what works and what does not. It is the magic of Harry Potter and the power of the dreams of Martin Luther King, Kennedy and Malala.

By the same token, advertising and propaganda deliberately exploit our susceptibility to story, to inform and change or influence opinion, feelings and

How our primitive DNA shapes moral behaviour   19

behaviour. When Steve Jobs launched the Mac and later the iPod and iPhone, he used story to sell the idea. He did not list the functions, features and benefits. When demagogues rouse crowds, they don't just recite a call to action, action is the inevitable outcome from the stories they weave.

We do not need to understand the biochemistry of how story works, we just need to harness its power.

1.13 The impotence of facts and logic to change opinion

Facts and logic are not sufficient to change opinions. In 2000, Brendan Nyhan and colleagues created a forum to correct untruths in claims made by politicians. What they discovered was that voters did not change their views even when presented with the lies told by politicians they supported. People's beliefs persist in spite of facts. Nothing has changed in the world of politics.

Researchers concluded that people have a tendency to adhere to misinformation that supports a political preference or aligns with their values or stereotype. Their support or opposition for political policies will depend on their broader alignment to a political view, not necessarily based on facts. Once people's cultural and political views get tied up in their factual beliefs, it's very difficult to undo, regardless of the messaging that is used.

Case study: political views

B Nyhan, J Reifler, PA Uble

Methods: We conducted an experiment to determine if more aggressive media fact-checking could correct the false belief that the Affordable Care Act in America would create 'death panels'. Participants from an opt-in Internet panel were randomly assigned to either a control group in which they read an article on Sarah Palin's claims about 'death panels' or an intervention group in which the article also contained corrective information refuting Palin.

Findings: The correction reduced belief in death panels and strong opposition to the reform bill among those who view Palin unfavorably and those who view her favorably but have low political knowledge. However, it backfired among politically knowledgeable Palin supporters, who were more likely to believe in death panels and to strongly oppose reform if they received the correction.

Conclusions: These results underscore the difficulty of reducing misperceptions about health care reform among individuals with the motivation and sophistication to reject corrective information.

20 *The human animal*

Case study: racial bias and perceptions of criminality

In another experiment, Professor Stephan Lewandowsky examined how racial bias impacted on the determination of guilt or innocence.

Participants were assessed for racial bias. They were then presented with a fictitious police report that surmised that the perpetrators of a robbery were aboriginal. After a short period, a new police report was issued which absolutely determined that the robbery was not committed by aboriginals. After a further interval during which participants performed unrelated tasks, the participants were asked who they thought committed the robbery. Those who were racially biased nominated aboriginals in spite of the facts being set out in the second police report.

The big questions that these studies raised were;

- Why does this happen? and
- What is the mechanism in the brain?

Case study: changing beliefs with electrical stimulation

A similar set of experiments was run, testing the impact of electrical stimulation on compliance behaviour. The conclusion of the scientists[6] goes some way to explain why facts and logic, which are processed in one part of the brain, do not change compliance behaviours, which occur in another.

All known human societies have maintained social order by enforcing compliance with social norms. The biological mechanisms underlying norm compliance are, however, hardly understood. We show that the right lateral prefrontal cortex (rLPFC) is involved in both voluntary and sanction-induced norm compliance. Both types of compliance could be changed by varying the neural excitability of this brain region with transcranial direct current stimulation, but they were affected in opposite ways, suggesting that the stimulated region plays a fundamentally different role in voluntary and sanction-based compliance. Brain stimulation had a particularly strong effect on compliance in the context of socially constituted sanctions, whereas it left beliefs about what the norm prescribes and about subjectively expected sanctions unaffected. Our findings suggest that rLPFC activity is a key biological prerequisite for an evolutionarily and socially important aspect of human behavior.

Conclusions from experimental research

Neuroscience has barely touched the surface of how beliefs are changed. Animal experiments have identified zones, precursors and specific neural activities associated with changes in the learned environment.

Some work has also been done in humans which indicates a similar localised area associated with changes in beliefs. Experiments have been carried out using external stimulation of the change zone. Not only did the behaviour change, but the polarity of the current impacted the direction of the change of belief. As yet there are no practical uses for this knowledge. Whether such intrusions would ever be deemed ethical is doubtful. Brainwashing would become brain current redirection. Frightening.

So, what do we know now?

- Factual and scientific evidence is often ineffective at reducing misperceptions. On highly emotive issues such as weapons of mass destruction, health care reform and vaccines, factual argument can backfire, reinforcing erroneous beliefs.
- More people know what scientists think about high-profile scientific controversies than polls suggest; they just aren't willing to endorse the consensus when it contradicts their political or religious views.
- Ideological (political) subgroups failed to update their beliefs when presented with corrective information that runs counter to their predispositions. Political activism is highest in those who believe in the need to be politically active to safeguard/promote their values and beliefs.
- Once people's cultural and political views get tied up in their factual beliefs, it's very difficult to undo, regardless of the messaging that is used.
- Racial beliefs determined opinions of guilt despite facts establishing innocence.

But change does occur.

- When a leader of the same affiliation (religious or political) endorsed the alternate facts. E.g. you can believe in human-induced climate change and still be a conservative Republican like former Representative Bob Inglis or an evangelical Christian like the climate scientist Katharine Hayhoe.
- When facts about the safety of vaccines (H1N1 and Influenza) were presented in discussion groups comprising parents, friends and spouse, changing beliefs was achieved more readily. The belief change triggered behavioural change and the inoculation rate increased.
- Politicians became more truthful when they were told and believed that 'fact checking' would impact their electability. They changed because there was a salient believable threat to things of value to them personally: reputation, standing, property and power.

22 *The human animal*

We have also witnessed the power of social, political and religious leaders to shape and change beliefs and behaviours of followers; to inspire, to attract more followers and to create a momentum that others wanted to join. The change can be positive like Roosevelt, Churchill and Kennedy, and destructive like Hitler, Pol Pot and genocidal leaders in Africa.

The development of virtual tribes and peers provides more areas for research. We have witnessed the power of social media to mobilise large numbers of people, but was this because people already had aligned beliefs, or were peer groups effecting changes in beliefs? Answering this question is urgent as the potential to manipulate beliefs, as distinct from manipulate believers, has enormous consequences for both harm and harm reduction.

1.14 Implications for ethics and behaviour training

Traditional corporate ethics and behaviour training relies on:

- Logic and reasoning;
- Imparting facts, knowledge and data through content-based training, especially e-learning;
- Communication of behavioural requirements through publication of formal values, policies and codes; and
- Presentation of case studies and scenarios.

These do not engage the non-conscious chemistry and hardwiring of our inherited biology, which is why the traditional approach fails. It is not just about knowledge. Effective behaviour change programmes tap into the power of:

- Our inherited primitive biology of survival, fear, belonging and trust;
- The leader and peers in the tribe, who keep us safe from harm, to create and enforce norms; and
- Story to encode the data to make it easier to assimilate.

Each of these is incorporated in Chapter 7, which summarises the major drivers that impact corporate behaviour.

Notes

1 In Haidt's model the closest pillars are reciprocity and care.
2 $w\Delta z = cov(wi,zi) + E(wi\Delta zi)$ is the equation developed by George Price which attempts to explain the evolution of altruism, applying Darwinian selection of the fittest traits.
3 Michael Regnier, https://mosaicscience.com/, 2017.
4 Yuval Harari, *Sapiens*, New York: HarperCollins, 2015.
5 Mike Lotzof, *Steve Jobs' Insights to Genius: 125 Powerful Lessons on Reinvention and Creativity*, Etram Publishing, 2012–2017.
6 CC Ruff, G Ugazio, E Fehr, Changing Social Norm Compliance with Non-invasive Brain Stimulation, *Science* 342, no. 6157: 482–484, 2013.

2 How beliefs, religion, ethics and the law shape behaviour

Key points:

- The evolution of societies from tribe to complex nation states required the development of tools of control beyond the brute physical power of the leader.
- All societies developed control systems founded on beliefs, religions and schools of ethical thought that crystallised in cultural norms, often formalised and entrenched in state issued and enforced laws.
- The determination of whether an action is right or wrong, good or bad, legal or illegal is thus dependent on the point in time and geography at which the determination is made.
- The interaction of different societies engendered an inevitable and irreconcilable clash of social control frameworks, being based in part on unprovable, but equally indisputable, belief systems.

Conclusion

- In a globalised, interconnected world, the determination of whether an action is right or wrong, good or bad, requires a system that is independent from the belief systems and entrenched laws of any particular society.

For the corporation

- Corporate behavioural codes that are derived from social systems will inevitably conflict with the values and belief systems of staff from other societies.
- Multinational corporations need a behavioural system that does not rely on the language of any one particular society or country.

24 *The human animal*

Anthropological research has established that over the millennia humans have engaged in religions, held complex belief systems, pursued the acquisition of property and the exercise of power. There have been leaders and followers. The evolution of social structures and political hierarchies, with associated promulgation and enforcement of rules and regulations, has provided a framework for growth and survival. We see variants of this model in the operation of nations, corporations and even street gangs.

Whether these behaviours are a necessary human condition, the outcome of evolutionary biology, or simply a product of custom and history, is not critical. What is central is to recognise that these elements – beliefs, property, power and control – exist, have shaped our ancestors and, even now, shape how we think and act. These forces, while influenced by our biology, are passed on not just through some immutable genetic inherited memory, but through the fluid systems and processes by which power, knowledge and insight grow and evolve, and are bequeathed from generation to generation.

> We live together because social organization provides the efficient means of achieving our individual objectives and not because society offers us a means of arriving at some transcendental common bliss. Politics is a process of compromising our differences, and we differ as to desired collective objectives just as we do over baskets of ordinary consumption goods.
>
> (James Buchanan)[1]

Philosophers have applied thought and logic, and even pseudo-science,[2] to interpret and frame how these elements of control should best be applied – to find a moral basis for our behaviour. Their influence on the models of jurisprudence has been profound. Philosophers are driven, in part, by a belief that our ability to reason, think abstractly and act logically is what distinguishes us from the lower species. They deny our biology.

Philosophers (and to a lesser degree lawyers) have striven to develop a single theory of morality that can be universally applied. They have failed. If human behaviour was simply a matter of logic and reason, it would be easy, but as set out in the previous chapter, people are not computers, and do not necessarily make decisions, and act, purely from logic and reason.

While our advanced brain function does make us superior, it does not immunise us from both the impact of our residual primitive brain function that drives fight, flight, fear and trust, nor the impact of faith and belief. Even while neuroscience (neurobiology and neurochemistry) reveals more about the non-logical, biological and physiological bases for behaviours, and reactions, philosophers still operate in the realms of logic and morality.

In Chapter 1 we addressed briefly the impact of innate and physiological response systems to understand why we act illogically. In this chapter, before

How beliefs, religion, ethics and the law shape behaviour   25

introducing the language of harm and the Harm Principles, we will examine the three major sources for setting standards and judging behaviour:

1. Belief, faith and religion
2. Philosophy and ethics
3. Law and regulation

2.1 Belief, faith and religions

Key points:

- There are two types of beliefs, those that are amenable to proof and disproof through the logical evaluation of facts, and those that are unprovable, such as faiths.
- Conflicts of beliefs cannot be resolved by rational or logical discussion.
- Beliefs have been used to develop and justify behavioural codes and often form the rationale for laws.
- Beliefs are powerful behavioural motivators that operate and persist notwithstanding contradictory fact and logic.
- Beliefs reside in a discrete part of the brain that is separate from other cognitive functions and the primal drivers.

Conclusion

- Beliefs and the language of beliefs cannot be used to develop a coherent set of universally usable behavioural guides that can be applied across national, cultural and demographic boundaries.
- Changing beliefs requires more than just knowledge and understanding.

For the corporation

- Changing behaviour requires more than the imposition, communication, teaching and enforcement of policies, procedures and codes of conduct.
- Addressing different belief systems and harnessing the power of beliefs is essential to effect control and drive change.

Behaviour is often driven by what people believe, as distinct from what they know. Beliefs have power, and because of this, it is vital to understand the nature of beliefs, the difference between belief and faith, and how faith

26 *The human animal*

manifests itself in organised religions with explicit codes of behaviour. Beliefs, faiths and religions shape not only individual actions, but have shaped, and continue to shape, societies, cultures, nations and the history of the world.

A corporation, being simply a special form of collective of people, is equally vulnerable to powerful belief systems, operating independently of the corporate controls and seemingly unsupported by fact or logic.

Beliefs

A belief is a state of mind in which a person holds an idea, conviction or tenet about an element of reality that may, or may not be, supported by evidence or fact. There are two sub-groups of beliefs: those to do with religion (faith), and those that deal with everything else (common beliefs).

Wherever the word belief is used in this book, it refers to common beliefs. The range of beliefs is limited only by the inventiveness of the human mind. Beliefs have influenced individual and public behaviour, often with catastrophic consequences.

Unlike religious faith, common beliefs are amenable to investigation, challenge, proof and disproof. At a given point in time, the subject of a particular belief may be unprovable, and thus unknowable. As technology and experience develops, beliefs have the intrinsic potential to morph into fact.

The scientific method of proposing a hypothesis (akin to, but not the same as, a belief), and then testing the hypothesis is the foundation of modern scientific knowledge. Once there is sufficient data, or evidence, the hypothesis could be proven or disproved. Knowledge converts hypothesis, or belief, into fact. The advance of science has disproved many false beliefs that were once held as unimpeachable truths. The two most profound being:

- The world is flat.
- The earth is the centre of the universe.

Both of these erroneous beliefs had sufficient power to have non-believers labelled heretics, and piously, and, very 'properly', executed. Beliefs in sorcery and black magic have caused people to tremble in fear, and witches and warlocks to be killed, often after torture.

> The difference between a belief masquerading as a truth, and a fact, is that facts can be established by investigation and analysis. What distinguishes a belief from knowledge, is that a belief, may be true, but still be unknown, residing in the twilight state of yet to be proven hypothesis.

- Belief in alien life is both unimpeachable and unprovable ... for now.

How beliefs, religion, ethics and the law shape behaviour 27

Things are only impossible until they are not.

(Jean Luc Picard, *Star Trek*)

The rapid acceleration of science continues to disprove beliefs and shibboleths. There is, however, a seemingly impenetrable frontier, where science encounters beliefs founded in religious dogma. This is best illustrated in the creation debate. There are two fundamental, mutually exclusive explanations of the origin of life on Earth, the creation of the Earth and how the universe came into being. Science-based analysis has developed the theory of evolution and the theory of the big bang. Enough data have been collected for evolution to move from theory to fact. The Big Bang remains a theory for now.

The empirically based evolution explanation for life on Earth is diametrically opposed to the religious-based model of creationists. The two systems are incompatible and cannot co-exist. Which one is deemed right, or wrong, depends purely on which belief system one follows. Scientists would point to the wealth of data they have uncovered, which is convincing, but not absolute, given that there are some gaps in the chain of proof.

What the argument on the creation of life on Earth illustrates is that conflict between belief systems allows a given situation to be simultaneously 'right and wrong', 'good and evil'. The determination will be dependent on the belief system of the persons making the judgement/decision, with profound implications for anyone on the wrong side of a belief, particularly those that have been enshrined in laws, with consequences for criminalisation and punishment.

Beliefs, therefore, are not a sound basis for developing a global framework to set standards and judge what is good or bad behaviour.

Faith and religions

Faith is a sub-set of beliefs, ordered around a deity or God. The faithful have an absolute, unprovable, but equally unshakeable acceptance in the existence and powers of some form of God, or supernatural being or beings. While people can passionately hold common beliefs, faith-based beliefs are often held with higher levels of conviction and certainty. Faith-based beliefs often form part of an individual's identity, making disagreement about the faith feel like an attack on their person.

The belief systems of the faithful are broad ranging, including concepts of existence and purpose, afterlife, heaven, hell, rebirth and karma. Gods can be singular, binary, a trilogy or multi-faceted. The Gods have powers to impact our lives positively and negatively. The favour of the Gods is sought by prayer, offerings and the performance of rituals as varied as the deity systems themselves.

Every religion has a code of behaviour, setting out the acceptable and proscribed; the consequence of non-adherence; the processes for seeking

28 *The human animal*

redemption, forgiveness and absolution; and the punishment for non-compliance. The faithful must accept and not challenge the prescriptions, for to do so brings into question the core articles of faith.

However, even faiths have proved mutable over time. Throughout history, challenges to the tenets of faith have taken place. Religions have evolved in form and substance, generating schisms and sects. These new sects, having faith in the absolute correctness of their approach and the fallacy of every other, have gone to war over their differences.[3] If sects of the same religion have fought each other, it is even easier to understand why different religions clash, with even greater vehemence, piety and certainty.

> We both pray to the same God for victory. How is this possible?[4]

Faiths pose a major dilemma for humanity. When faith is so profound that it inhibits acceptance of other faiths, or the acceptance of scientific and empirically proven facts, conflict will be inevitable. The expression 'blind faith' implies that the faithful disregard any evidence that may run counter to a central tenet.

> As hatred is defined as intense dislike, what is wrong with inciting intense dislike of a religion, if the activities or teachings of that religion are so outrageous, irrational or abusive of human rights that they deserve to be intensely disliked?
>
> (Rowan Atkinson)

Theists argue that without a belief in God there is no foundation upon which to build a moral code that is not malleable, bending to the whim of society. They argue that the metaphysical basis is needed to keep man in line.

While they acknowledge that non-believers (other religions, or atheists) aren't implicitly immoral, they argue that there is a need for a higher source for an objective, moral code. The power of God to punish, a God who sees all, but forgives in certain circumstances, is a powerful force for shaping behaviour.

Gods may be sufficient for imposing control for the deeply faithful, but for the marginal believer and in a multi-faith globalised world, the power of God to punish, on Earth or in a future life, is of questionable value as a temporal guiding force. Furthermore, deeply religious people of all denominations have committed crimes against societal norms and prevailing laws and even against their own religious cannon. It is easy to reframe Dostoyevsky, who said in The Brothers Karamazov,

> If God is dead, all is permitted, Even if God exists, evil will be perpetrated, even by the Godly.

Another fatal flaw for proponents of theistic systems as the basis for global temporal law is that different religions over time have encoded and enforced

How beliefs, religion, ethics and the law shape behaviour   29

barbaric, inhuman and amoral laws, at least when viewed through a modern lens. Some examples illustrate the inadequacy of theistic systems.

- Innumerable wars have been fought – one religion against another, both claiming God as their own and on their side.
- Fundamentalist Christian, Muslim and Jewish sects all impose restrictions and limitations on the civil and legal rights and personal power of women.
- Inconvenient precepts set out in the literal interpretation of the Bibles and Koran require severe punishment, including death, stoning, maiming for various crimes such as homosexuality, blasphemy, failing to keep the Sabbath and adultery.

The fact that religious laws vary over time, even within one religion, suggests that religions derive their moral laws from humans, not the other way around.

Proponents of religious tolerance argue correctly that there are many shared values across different religions. These values have often found their way into criminal and civil laws. By extension, they argue that religions are therefore valuable in forming the basis for a universal code of behaviour. There is no question that religious precepts have formed and continue to form the basis of many laws. This, however, is more by evolutionary coincidence than by divine design.

Religions do not provide a fungible base for a universal code for our complex, rapidly changing globalised world for two primary reasons:

- Religions contradict each other over what is moral/right/wrong; and
- Within one religion, what is moral/right/wrong changes over time.

The situation may be best summarised by Groucho Marx, who said:

These are my principles. If you don't like them I have others.

Perhaps the most damning fatal flaw in the claim that religions should be the source of a universal, globally usable code for behaviour is the potential for extreme fundamentalists to establish rules and codes that are inherently draconian, intolerant and discriminatory.

Though I am a strong advocate for free thought on all subjects, yet it appears to me (whether rightly or wrongly) that direct arguments against Christianity or Theism produce hardly any effect on the public, and freedom of thought is best promoted by the gradual advancement of science. It has, therefore, always been my object to avoid writing on religion, and I have confined myself to science.

(Charles Darwin)

30   *The human animal*

The impact of belief and faith on decision making and behaviour

> Faith, as well intentioned as it may be, must be built on facts, not fiction –
> faith in fiction is a damnable false hope.
>
> (Thomas A. Edison)

The critical common distinguishing feature of both faith and common belief-based systems is that they do not rely on evidence, proof or rational analysis. The impact can be severe. Beliefs can be fervently held, based on nothing more than a rumour, or superstition, often perpetuated over generations. For example, stereotypes based on an individual's religion, race, sex or age often shape how a person is perceived to be, regardless of the facts. Classes of people are labelled as stingy, lazy, criminally inclined, smart or sexy because of stereotypical beliefs, not facts.

Parents, across cultures, have told stories of the bogeyman, harnessing fear, with the intent of frightening children into behaving properly. The bogeyman has taken many forms: the short Tokeloshe man of Southern Africa; El Cuco of Spain; the Busseman of Germany. Each society uses a belief system to manipulate behaviour – in this case for relatively benign motives – to get kids, and in some cultures adults, to behave as society dictates.

However, belief-based behaviour and decision models are vulnerable to manipulation. The most sinister manipulation of beliefs results in genocides. Races, religions and native populations were demonised, or deemed sub-human, justifying the perpetration of slavery, mass slaughter, confiscation of property and appropriation of land. Dehumanisation is the foundation of the doctrine of Terra Nullius, which allowed continents like Australia to be legally occupied and its Aboriginal people dispossessed, hunted and killed.

Civil wars and wars of conquest and colonisation have nearly always had a belief-based justification to gain public support. The conquered are demonised and dehumanised, masking the real motives of securing or preserving resources, the accumulation of wealth, the enhancement of power, the spreading of faiths and the 'saving' of souls.

When belief-based dehumanisation is twinned with the destruction of social controls and norms, the descent to barbarism is inevitable, as tribalism and fear of others is given free reign. The turbulence caused by the self-styled Islamic State is not unique to Islam: it is the logical outcome of conflict generated by belief systems for which right and wrong, acceptable and unacceptable, equal and inferior are based on fervently held faiths, tribalism and ethnicity.

Institutionalising belief in difference

The persuasive and coercive power of difference is ultimately manifested in written and unwritten laws that govern tribes and societies. Part of the process of

How beliefs, religion, ethics and the law shape behaviour   31

building a strong society has been to institutionalise and codify these differences. We have woven them into our mythology, and passed them down, generation to generation, underpinned by our DNA and reinforced by our inherited primitive survival biology.

Codification of mythology has been used by the empowered to justify their position, and, contrarily, even by the oppressed to help them justify why they meekly accept their fate and position in life. A few examples are sufficient to illustrate the point:

1. Beliefs in the superiority of the ruling classes, and the converse inferiority of lower classes, races and castes, has led to institutionalised ill-treatment: apartheid, slavery, caste, sex slavery and child labour. Each has been justified by societies and by laws.
2. Beliefs in the superiority of certain races and religions have made it easy to justify war, appropriation of lands and even extermination. They were the origin of the Crusades and Islamic holy wars. In America and Australia there was widespread genocide (before it was a popularised term) and appropriation of lands by the early white settlers. In all of these, the others (enemy) were denigrated, demonised and made sub-human. These beliefs are the foundation for 'moral' wars and have been used to ennoble killing.
3. Belief that democracy should be 'imposed or gifted', even by war, on societies that may not have the institutional capacity, cultural foundations or belief in individual equality necessary for democracy to work.
4. Homosexuals are criminals.
5. Tribal differences in Rwanda, Zimbabwe and Syria.
6. Religious tribal differences in Ireland, Somalia, Lebanon and Bosnia
7. Sectarian differences in Syria and Iraq.
8. Belief that the democratically elected majority can impose their will on the minority.
9. The market knows best and is self-correcting.

In each of the above examples, there is an institutionalised belief system, usually codified in laws, and quite often founded on a religious platform, which allows those in power to operate, believing they are doing nothing wrong. They are self-righteous.

Implicitly, those who break the law, or even have the temerity to exist, should be punished, and certainly not allowed access to the good things in life, except if they kowtow to the empowered.

Beliefs and the corporation

Corporations are fully attuned to exploiting the vulnerabilities of customer belief systems, yet are singularly inept at incorporating this knowledge of belief

32 *The human animal*

systems into their day-to-day and strategic management of the internals of the organisation.

Marketing gurus carefully tune product and branding messages to the specifics of each demographic – race, colour, creed, culture, socio-economic grouping, literacy, numeracy. They know that the messages must align with the differences in language, custom and beliefs of their target market, yet internal corporate policies and other control materials are a uniform vanilla, flavoured with a heavy sprinkling of legalese and political correctness. Too often they ignore the local world view. They decry the intransigence of far-flung outposts (anyone not in the head office). How often have you heard the cries of exasperation? 'Why don't *they* get it?'

Messages from the ivory tower are therefore often:

- Ignored;
- Reinterpreted;
- Selectively used;
- Derided for their 'irrelevance' and 'lack of understanding' of the local market;
- Not necessarily acted on as intended.

Complex ideas are consistently published by multi-national and multi-cultural corporations only in the 'official language'. This further dilutes the transfer of meaning and understanding. The outcome is increased disengagement and distrust that the head office knows, understands or even cares about the local outpost. This mismatching results from two sets of conflicting beliefs – the head office and the local.

Head offices:

- Know they are right;
- Believe they:

  - Are the only ones who can see the big picture;
  - Understand the strategic vision;
  - Understand the global regulatory risks;
  - Are the true brand ambassadors and protectors;

- Believe the locals are:

  - Wilful renegades;
  - Stupid;
  - Uneducated;
  - Less experienced;
  - Less exposed to the real world.

Local offices:

- Believe they:
  - Understand their local issues better than head office;
  - Know what is best locally;
  - Know how to apply policies to local conditions to remain competitive;
- Believe head office:
  - Lives in the clouds;
  - Is unrealistic and detached from the real world;
  - Should not force global standards on local operations.

All of these are real descriptors from workshops, held on every continent except Antarctica. What the lists illustrate is a conflict of beliefs, with a consequent destruction of trust. When things go wrong, head offices typically respond by increasing the controls, especially issuing more policies, organising more training and often 'parachuting' in someone who 'gets it'. They do not look at conflicts of beliefs, the nature of human biology, or the perceived leadership invisibility on these issues.

Issuing more controls of the same typology does nothing to address the belief systems conflicts. More of the same exacerbates the lack of trust.

> *Insanity is* doing the same thing over and over again and expecting different results.
>
> (Albert Einstein)

The consequences are clear:

- If we do not trust the systems of controls (or in society – law and justice), then we may decide to act outside the controls (make our own law and justice).
- If we have belief systems that run counter to behaviours that are being imposed by the corporate controls (or societal laws), we may resist or ignore the requirement.

In both situations, the actors feel justified that what they are doing is right and what is being required of them is wrong. It is their belief in what is 'right and wrong' as defined by the tribe with which they really identify which needs to be understood and managed when trying to influence and shape behaviour.

> Just because staff have the same employer, one paymaster, one logo and all the standard corporate trappings, does not make them feel like they belong to one tribe.

34 *The human animal*

We also need to harness the biological mechanism identified in Chapter 1 to realign parallel belief systems that distort behaviour. Some of the well-entrenched corporate beliefs that can distort behaviour include:

- Profit is the only role of business and can be pursued at any cost;
- The sanctity of targets;
- Bonuses drive behaviour;
- Bonuses are a right, especially if it is in my contract;
- All is fair in business;
- Might is right;
- Loyalty is right – blowing the whistle on wrong-doing is bad;
- Absolute adherence to orders;
- Them and us silo-tribes across products, countries and regions;
- Them and us between hierarchies;
- It was legal, so what is the problem? I did nothing wrong.

The war crimes defence – 'I was only following orders' – was offered to explain, or justify, barbaric behaviour. It is impossible to see into the minds of those offering the plea, but it is quite possible, if not probable, that while loyally following orders, they were also acting out deeply held tribal beliefs on difference that had been deeply inculcated and invisiblised, reappearing as profound behaviour-guiding truths.

While drawing a comparison between war criminals with business practices may seem extreme, the damage done by the staff and leaders of businesses, who believed in their right to do what they did, has been substantial. Examples include:

- Cancer caused by smoking where executives knew and covered up the danger;
- Cancer caused by asbestos, long after the danger was known;
- Contamination of air, land and water by release of toxic chemicals, either as part of a manufacturing process or through uncontrolled disposal;
- Damage caused by companies using their power and financial strength to defend cases where culpability was clear;
- Selling financial products to people, knowing they were unsuitable;
- The global financial crisis.

Conclusions

- Beliefs have no role as a basis for a system to guide behaviour in our globalised, multi-cultural, interconnected world; and
- To change behaviour, we need to address the core belief systems, replacing destructive beliefs with productive beliefs. This cannot be achieved by logic and content. We must address the biology and hereditary behavioural mechanisms as well, wrapped in a powerful story.

2.2 Ethics, logic, morality and values

Key points:

- Ethics and values are specific and valid for the group that created and adheres to them.
- Differing group ethical and behavioural norms and expectations are equally valid for each group.
- Resolving conflicts of ethics cannot be achieved using logic or the standard language of ethics or claims of superiority of one set of group values over another.

Conclusion

- Ethics and values systems are useful to describe group behaviours, but do not provide a tool for guiding behaviours across national, cultural and demographic boundaries, or where groups have differing values systems.

For the corporation

- Having all staff behave in accordance with an agreed set of values is important for control, to build internal and external trust and to avoid community and regulatory backlash.
- The effectiveness of ethics and values programmes is limited by conflicts of values (corporate, national, local and individual) and by the limitation of standard ethical language, to make the corporate values resonate for each individual.
- The language of Harm provides a more effective basis for imparting the meaning and impact of the corporate values to the individual.

I begin with an apology to ethicists and moral philosophers, who for centuries have debated right and wrong, the roots from which right and wrong spring, and the nuances of when something that is defined as wrong may not be wrong, depending on the circumstances. Societies place considerable store in people acting ethically and morally. Or in simpler terms, in accordance with the prevailing behavioural norms.

Norms specify the range of permissible actions in a given situation, whether as mundane as dress codes and manners, to the more weighty, governing collective cooperation, bilateral agreement and complying with laws. Norms are considered the defining difference between our civilized human society and animals. To

36 *The human animal*

reinforce our superiority and to help stability, societies have turned to philosophers and ethicists to develop codes that can be lived by, and which explain why things are right or wrong.

There is a great deal of semantics involved in this topic. Words such as ethics, morals, values and principles are used. To the non-specialist, which is the overwhelming majority of the world, the differences are irrelevant. We just want to know what can and can't we do? Without splitting hairs and delving into the nuanced differences, it is useful to get a feel for these commonly used words even though the practical difference between ethics and morality is blurred. The dominant view is that ethics is simply the abstract study of the sets of rules which define whether the behaviour is acceptable (moral).

Ethics is formally defined as:

- A system of moral principles: e.g. the ethics of a culture.
- The rules of conduct recognised in respect of a particular class of human actions or a particular group, culture, etc. e.g. medical ethics; Christian ethics.
- Moral principles, as of an individual: e.g. His ethics forbade betrayal of a confidence.
- That branch of philosophy dealing with values relating to human conduct, with respect to the rightness and wrongness of certain actions and to the goodness and badness of the motives and ends of such actions. [5]

Morality, by contrast, is commonly used in anthropology and sociology to codify, compare and contrast the ethics, values, norms or codes of conduct of different societies and groups, whether they are primitive tribes, criminal gangs, religious groups or even business cabals.

Morals (or norms) are simply the principles that determine how one should act in a particular context. The moral set could be created by a group, such as a religion or political cadre, or defined by an individual. We are familiar with the expression of a 'personal code'. This code may not align to the group's and that person is said to be guided by their personal moral compass. We often call these our values, which is not the same as what we value. Confusing!

This sufficiently illustrates the problems of these semantic differences for the average person and staff of corporations. The useful common thread is that each deals with concepts that guide behaviour. Whether these forces are called ethics, values, principles or rules is an irrelevant semantic nicety. What is important is that a set of ideas exists, which shape and define what behaviours are acceptable or unacceptable. The ideas become the reference point against which a group can determine if a specific action is good or bad, right or wrong, i.e. if it is OK!

Once the labels are sorted, the outcome can be disquieting. What is good and bad, right and wrong is dependent on whatever set of principles is accepted by the group. What is ethical in one group may well be unethical in another. Morality is thus relative. Regardless of the strength of an individual's personal moral compass, following it in a different moral world will lead to the abyss of breaching local morality.

How beliefs, religion, ethics and the law shape behaviour 37

While philosophers, and ethicists in particular, have codified, deconstructed and rebuilt systems of ethics, they have failed to generate any kind of approach that is effective across divergent groups and cultural boundaries. Philosophers are great at describing what exists in each area but have failed at uncovering a unifying universal ethic or approach that transcends differences between cultures, societies and nations. They do a great job in pointing out what the common threads are and what the differences are, and even explore the origins and forces that drive difference.

This is not a philosophy text, and the analysis of the myriad schools of thought is beyond the scope of this book; however, it is interesting to glance at a few schools of Western ethical thought. The first school deals in the concept of *virtues*, as first articulated by Aristotle (justice, charity, generosity, etc); the second revolves around principles of *the duty of rational beings to respect each other*, as propounded by Kant and his followers; the third, based on the works of Mill, is based on *the primacy of happiness of the greatest number – utilitarianism*. Each of these has influenced how we think about human interactions and our own conduct. But the critical question is, do they provide a basis for a framework in our globalised world?

Aristotle believed that simply knowing what was right would guide a person to do right; that evil is a function of ignorance of self and consequence. Aristotle was manifestly incorrect. Many who break codes, whether criminal or social, generally do so with full knowledge of what they are doing, and the consequences of their actions. What Aristotle may have been observing was the power of Athenian society to impose its values, however they were derived. He was a victim of inductive reasoning.

Egalitarianism favours equality, advocating the removal of inequalities among people. Clearly, the Western world has failed at implementing this precept given the increasing wealth disparities in societies – regardless of hemisphere. Egalitarianism conflicts with Libertarianism. The libertarian extolls freedom, individual liberty, voluntary association and respect of property rights, which may not be distributed equally. They decry big government and go so far as to call taxation theft. Libertarianism aligns well with the disparities of modern society and is one of the founding values used to justify our current social order and the increasing divergence in wealth and wellbeing.

Utilitarianism suggests that the proper course of action is the one that maximizes the overall 'happiness' benefits for the majority. This implicitly justifies the tyranny of the majority at the expense of the minority.

No one school is adequate. Each has appeal, but they fail, even when conjoined, to form a basis for guiding human behaviour, particularly as globalisation makes the world more complex.

The values veil

Regardless of the source, we each develop a set of values that guides us – our moral compass. But unlike the physical world, with one magnetic north, the

38 *The human animal*

moral world has multiple norths that vary by country, city, family and even the organisation we work for. We are all exposed to multiple value sets on a daily basis. What values we apply at home may differ from those when out with friends, or those required at work.

The impact on individual responses is complex. We don't simply abandon one set of values for another, depending on context, or do we?

How we respond to situations where multiple sets of values operate is a continuum. At one end of the spectrum, we can select one set and ignore other conflicting value sets. For example, teenage gangs, who do not like certain socially prescribed values ignore them and form their own set. They rebel, reject and replace. It is not that they are without values; it is just that the socially imposed values set is ignored, and their new adopted value set is adhered to, even while they continue to live within society. The potential for problems arises when their gang-value driven behaviours conflict with what is expected in their society. It is not a new phenomenon: youthful rebellion was commented on by Plato.

> What is happening to our young people? They disrespect their elders, they disobey their parents. They ignore the law. They riot in the streets inflamed with wild notions. Their morals are decaying. What is to become of them?
>
> (Plato – *The Republic*)

The phenomenon Plato described is the simultaneous rejection of one set of values and their replacement by new values. Within the construct of the gang, every gang member is expected to live by the gang's values and demonstrate the expected behaviours. The new set of values is internalised, providing the scale for judging what is right and wrong, good or bad, at least, while having intra-gang interactions.

The world, however, is not a simple dichotomy between the establishment and youthful rebellion. The interaction between value sets is rarely binary and mutually exclusive. There is potential for simultaneous alignment and conflict. The twentieth century witnessed peaceniks, environmentalists, love-ins, flower power and anti-war pacifism, simultaneously with communism, fascism, McCarthyism, conservative reactionaries, progressive socialists; the right to life and pro-choice; equal rightists supporting, variously, women, blacks, gay marriage and a spectra of religions.

In the simplistic gang example given in this section, there is an artificially forced choice – one set or another. In reality, it is more common that we are required to behave with multiple value sets that operate sequentially and sometimes simultaneously. For the most part, the value sets are aligned, with resolvable and limited conflicts. For example, each of us deals with several contextual value sets;

- At home with family;
- At work with colleagues and customers;

How beliefs, religion, ethics and the law shape behaviour 39

- Out socially with friends;
- As a voluntary member of an association: religion, social/sports club; and
- Living in the community – neighbours, people providing goods and services, and strangers.

Corporations need to understand how staff transition from private life to corporate values. On arrival at work, employees are expected to don the corporate Values Veil, which they are required to wear and live by in all things expected at work. The veil is chosen as a metaphor because it recognises two factors. A veil can have degrees of transparency, recognising that the employee's values still exist below the veil and second that the corporate values are applied 'lightly', recognising the continued operation of the individual's values.

The exercise of personal values is moderated by the corporation's values, but not eliminated. A common example is gender discrimination. In private life, treating females poorly may be the norm, but in the Western corporate world it would technically be prohibited, but is too often condoned.

Where the values are aligned, the employee can wear the veil lightly. On arrival at work, the Values Veil is relatively transparent, allowing the employee to behave in the work environment in a way that is consistent with the way the person would behave at home, or with friends, because there is no conflict. The employees with aligned values need not abandon 'who they are', as they sign in.

However, when work and private values conflict, the veil becomes heavier and the employee will feel the weight and discomfort of doing things that are required at work but do not sit comfortably. The discomfort will generate dissonance. The impact on behaviours and feelings will range from silent stoicism to complaining at home, to outright refusal to do the 'wrong' or 'stupid' thing, even if it is required by the corporation.

Ultimately, if the conflict of values is profound, the employee may resign to avoid being forced to do the wrong thing, or be fired for failing to adhere to corporate policy.

For corporations, and for employees, one of the critical success factors for engaged employees is to ensure that hiring is not just about a match of experience, talent and skills, but also an alignment of values. It is critical to recognise the mechanism of the corporate Values Veil and the underlying personal values, and how the two sets of values will interact and impact on behaviour and motivation.

The potential of values to guide individual behaviour breaks down if values violations are not sanctioned. Employees tend to follow prevailing values, provided they witness values compliance by others. This is true in all human societies. Every society has enforced norm compliance by threatening violators with punishment. The effectiveness of enforcement of sanctions has been established in cultural studies and is supported by evolutionary biology and research experiments.

40 *The human animal*

The morality mask

There is another state, beyond the Values Veil, called the Morality Mask. The Morality Mask comes into being when the corporate values are so internalised that they dominate, suppressing the operation of any other values systems that the employee may have held.

The difference between the Values Veil and the Morality Mask is fundamental. The Values Veil permits the coexistence of aligned, but different, values systems. The Morality Mask demands total alignment, excluding the operation of all conflicting values systems. In a mask state, the values are so internalised that they are indistinguishable from the psyche of the person. The very identity of the person is defined by the mask.

The Morality Mask imbues the wearer with moral certainty. The masked feel good, and fully justified, to the point of wanting to bind others to join a group of the like-minded.

Masks may be beneficial or harmful, depending on the values set. It is hard to argue with apparently benign values, fervently upheld, such as a religious order dedicated to peace and charity. The problem with the mask state is that it makes wearers vulnerable to the whims of the leaders. The tragic results in cults have been well documented.

History is littered with righteous, mask-wearing believers perpetrating despicable evil on people who were categorised as different. The righteous, holding dear to their values, promulgated laws, social norms and taboos and then enforced them with zealous policing and judicial practices. Morality masks allow harmful actions to be swathed in a righteous cloak.

The list is too long to pick a worst case that best illustrates the point. How do you differentiate righteous crusades, inquisitions, fatwas and jihads; the demonization of witches, warlocks, gays, communists and capitalist running dogs; the killing fields of Cambodia and Rwanda; the Nazi concentration camps, Russian and Chinese re-education centres; and the multi-generational genocides of anti-Semitic pogroms?

The so called 'modern civilised world' is not immune. We celebrate the end to immoral tyrannies, the end to slavery and child labour, and the right to vote for women, people of colour and Aborigines for the true victories they were, but fail to stop the next wave – a different time, a different place, a different victim typology, but the same pathology. We wring our hands and stand by doing little and even nothing. We do no active harm, but, by doing little, facilitate those who would inflict harm.

What is it in the human pathology that allows us to repeatedly descend into the abys of righteous evil, or in business, join in with the 'immoral' collective? Why do we drink the Kool Aid and then encourage others to do the same? How do we create Nazi death-camp guards, who lovingly kiss their children goodbye and then club the children of others to death?

It is the myth-powered mask drawing on our most primitive biology.

Masks also appear in the corporate world. Corporate leaders have been known to demand total, unquestioning loyalty. They generate cult-like, blind adherence.

How beliefs, religion, ethics and the law shape behaviour   41

There is a fine line between loyalty and motivation, which permit free thought about the correctness of actions, and a mask state which silences dissent, often instilling fear in those who want to raise issues.

Corporate mask states inhibit internal feedback of identified problems. Those who want to raise issues are forced outside, to vent their grievances in the media or with regulators.

Creating a mask

The internal mechanisms of how values morph into masks are complex and not well understood. Why will one identical twin brother be radicalised and the other not?

While we do not understand the exact process, we can observe the process in operation and the impact on behaviour. The Veil solidifies into a Mask, which fuses into the fabric of the member. Identity is lost and the individual is absorbed into the Borg[6]-like collective. This is different from wearing a mask as a disguise to avoid identification.

Each collective has its own rules, based on a code or values, as varied as the Ku Klux Klan, bike and drug gangs, or the self-styled Islamic State. Trust between mask wearers is built on absolute adherence to the values of the group. What is critical to appreciate is that trust is independent of the values set. Trusting is about alignment.

Resistance is futile.

Fear, belonging, tribalism and biology

The genetic origin of masks probably has its roots in the primitive drive to belong in order to survive. We belonged to the collective because it could hunt, gather and defend itself more effectively than an individual. There is most likely a region of the brain that supports belonging to a group and supporting collective behaviour because those without the collective belonging drive would be less likely to survive. By corollary, individuals with a higher collective drive, the fittest, would dominate the reproductive chain. The neurochemistry of trust[7] reinforces belonging by mask wearers as they indulge in their rituals and ceremony.

The need to belong is a powerful force, capable of overriding logic and reason. Elderly Jews have described how as children they wanted to join the Hitler Youth and the Italian Black shirts. They were angry and felt betrayed when their parents would not permit it. At the time, they did not understand or accept that the marching gangs they so wanted to be part of would have excluded them from belonging.

Masks are extraordinarily powerful. They subvert and replace all other value systems. A common trait of mask wearers is their penchant to dehumanise and

42 *The human animal*

demonise those who are different, who do not fit, and in so doing reinforce their own collective identity – where they belong. Mask wearing is the ultimate state of belonging.

In its mildest form, we see masks emerge in schools – the in-crowd and the losers, the jocks and the nerds. Some individuals balance internal and external value sets, but others subsume their internal compass in favour of the group's values. They don the mask and all its appurtenances – dress, language and codes of behaviour.

Our complex modern societies no longer operate on simple survival collectives. However, the innate collective drive has not disappeared, like our simian tail. Our physical evolution has been outpaced by our social and economic evolution. As a consequence, many of our behavioural rules (laws, norms) seem to operate to hold in check the expression of our innate survival drivers. Holding a driver in check, however, is not the same as eliminating it.

Mask-wearing tribalism is alive and well and living in the hearts of fanatical sports fans who vicariously do battle by proxy. Masks find expression in partisan party political supporters, who while trotting out the mantra and creed, rarely understand the fundamental logic. How many Tea Party and Alt-Right adherents truly understand the logic of policies and positions? The same could be said for extreme socialists, capitalists, market adherents, globalisers and climate change alarmists. Logic gives way to beliefs that align with belonging. Values realign to support belonging.

Capitalist and socialist tribes ardently espouse their own doctrines, fervently denouncing and demonising the others. 'Better dead than red!' was a popular cry of the 1950s. The late Fidel Castro professed, 'Socialism or death'. The vehemence and hatred is not logical, nor is it, in modern society, existential. This does not stop leaders playing to the threat to 'our way of life' to garner support by triggering the primitive survival collective driver. The same fervour has seen misguided attempts to transplant (impose) democratic values on societies more accustomed to dictatorships and tribal leadership, whose codes and myths are more aligned and in tune with command and control.

The ultimate tribal myth finds expression as the nation state. Nationalism is a prime source of values. The more fervent and extreme the form of mythology around nationalism, the more powerful the mask becomes to distort and control behaviour. World War II was a time of existential nationalism. It was sufficiently powerful to temporarily overcome gender, religious and racial barriers. Women worked in factories. Military regiments were integrated. The differences were reluctantly papered over to serve the collective need to survive until the existential threat was over and things could return to 'normal' and entrenched values reassert themselves.

Religion is one of the primary sources of masks. As discussed before, theistic beliefs are not amenable to logic or reason. They are taken on faith. The step from faithful to blind followship is relatively small. Profound faith, like political belief, coupled with tribal belonging, enables charismatic, story-wielding religious leaders to generate momentum and an evangelical following – beneficial, benign or destructive.

The essential difference between the Veil and the Mask is one of degree. When wearing the mask, the individual absorbs all of the values or morals of the mask and then acts without question or reservation. Certainty is comforting. Masks always embrace intrinsic sanctions. Peer, social, financial and fear control mechanisms are common tools for enforcing and maintaining alignment. There is overt and covert coercion, which is of itself seen as not just acceptable, but necessary. Slogans encapsulate and clarify.

- You are with us or against – us v. them (others);
- For the good of the entity;
- Never leave a man behind.

The mask also trades on traditional values and traits, but takes them to extremes.

- Loyalty;
- Response to leadership and authority;
- Desire to belong;
- Reciprocity.

Conclusion

There is no single set of ethics or values that can be used as a global guide for behaviour. Ethics and morality are contextual, changing with time, place and the distribution of power. The failure to identify a common thread makes it difficult for globalised corporations to develop a single moral or ethical code that is universally accepted. This does not help the CEO trying to set the code of practice for a multi-national to communicate to all staff:

What is the meaning of GOOD?

While, on the surface, corporations appear to be just a group of people and, as such, subject to similar behaviour controls as natural groups and societies, corporations are in fact made more complex because of their legal nature, purpose and structure.

Notwithstanding the forgoing, corporations continue to invest in developing and promoting values systems based on traditional ethical language, as part of their behavioural control mechanisms. They assume their values will be adopted just because they are promulgated in a glossy brochure with the corporate logo and signature of the chairman.

Making values relevant and lived is discussed in Chapter 8.

44 *The human animal*

2.3 Law, power and the lawyer's duty

Key points:

- An action is illegal simply because it contravenes a law, not because the action is inherently bad or harmful.
- Laws are created to reflect the views of those in control.
- Laws differ depending on the location and time in history.
- At any one time the same action can be legal and illegal depending on the jurisdiction.
- The legal system rewards those who can find the gaps in the law so that they can act legally, even though the action is harmful.

Conclusion

- The law is not a sound basis for guiding global behaviour.

For the corporation

- Obeying the law is at best a minimum set of standards.
- Finding the gap in laws is a legal corporate activity, but exploiting gaps in the law sets up future liability if the action is inherently harmful. Ultimately, the law will be changed.
- Those who received the short-term benefit from exploiting a gap in the law may well have 'moved on', leaving the liability for rectification to their successors and, ultimately, shareholders.
- A corporate culture that rewards pursuing gaps in the law negatively impacts adherence to corporate controls. Staff will also look for and exploit gaps in control systems such as policies, codes and values, shading interpretation to justify a course of action.

The role of laws

Laws are created to help regulate the operation of our society. The more complex the society, the more complex the suite of laws. Laws are necessary to protect the less able, and the less powerful, from being exploited by the powerful and unscrupulous.

> Laws are partly formed for the sake of good men, in order to instruct them how they may live on friendly terms with one another, and partly for the

How beliefs, religion, ethics and the law shape behaviour   45

sake of those who refuse to be instructed, whose spirit cannot be subdued, or softened, or hindered from plunging into evil.

(Plato)

Earlier in this chapter we discussed the limitation of beliefs and values in providing a universal guide for setting behavioural standards, because beliefs and values:

- Vary over place and time;
- Do not allow for logical resolution of conflicts between differing belief and values systems; and
- Are open to distortions that allow the pious and righteous to justify *behaving badly.*

Laws occupy an unusual position that distinguishes them from belief and ethical systems. Laws embody the power of the State. Laws demand adherence because trial and punishment await those who break them. This power was once the province of religious and tribal/village leaders, who upheld religious and customary laws, which were often based on faith, beliefs and values that had evolved over time. The system worked because of the relative isolation and homogeneity of the communities.

The very heart of legal systems is based on one simple precept: an act is illegal, or criminal, simply because it contravenes a law. Being illegal is not the same as being wrong because, as discussed in the previous sections, right and wrong are contextual, depending on where and who you are at a given point in time.

The sanctity and power of the law and the legal system raises many contrarian issues. Abraham Lincoln fought a political and civil war and gave his life to change the right to own slaves – a law that divided nations, yet Lincoln viewed even bad laws as sacred, requiring adherence to preserve the integrity of the society.

Let me not be understood as saying that there are no bad laws, nor that grievances may not arise for the redress of which no legal provisions have been made. I mean to say no such thing. But I do mean to say that although bad laws, if they exist, should be repealed as soon as possible, still, while they continue in force, for the sake of example they should be religiously observed.

(Abraham Lincoln)

Lincoln understood that to avoid the corruption of society, its legislature, police and judiciary, it is necessary to not only adhere to a bad law but also to accept the consequences for breaching the bad law. This seems bizarre but is a necessary requirement if the rule of law is to persist. The alternative is anarchy.

46　*The human animal*

The origin of laws

> Whoever desires to found a state and give it laws, must start with assuming that all men are bad and ever ready to display their vicious nature, whenever they may find occasion for it.
>
> (Niccolo Machiavelli)

In democracies, we think of laws as:

- Rules that govern behaviour; that are
- Created by a democratically elected governing body; whose actions are
- Consistent with the governing constitution (written, or traditional); and the laws are
- Policed by independent agencies; and
- Culpability for breach of laws is determined by an independent judiciary.

Even in the most primitive societies aspects of these five elements have been identified, though the degree of democracy, the independence of policing and the judiciary would vary, reflecting the structure of the society at that time.

In dictatorships and sham democracies, laws are often created to entrench the powers of the elite, including the distribution and accumulation of wealth. This distortion of behaviour is exacerbated when there is absolute control of policing and judiciary.

Rarely are laws accepted by society as an immutable whole. Whether laws started as simply as, say, the Ten Commandments or as complex as Napoleon's Civil Code, the originals will invariably be modified over time as societies' values change. At any point in time, it is highly likely that, at least for a section of the community, there will be a conflict between the law and individual faith, beliefs and ethical values.

The forces for changing laws are diverse, ranging from the subtle, building over time, to the catastrophic, which generates a ground swell for immediate revolutionary change. The underlying forces for change include:

- Inequality – changes in the relative economic prosperity of groups within society;
- Growth – economic and populations;
- Beliefs – the evolving norms and mores of society, including the construct of human rights;
- Structure – changes in the mix of classes and strata;
- Education – the growth of empirical knowledge supplanting superstition and beliefs;
- Complexity – trade, products;
- Advances in science, technology and communications;
- Globalisation – the change in patterns of trade, migration and flows of capital;

How beliefs, religion, ethics and the law shape behaviour 47

- The diminution of the autonomy and power of the nation state; and
- The rise in power of multi-national organisations – both commercial and political.

This is not an exhaustive list, but it illustrates that there are many forces and currents that challenge the adequacy of the laws in place at a point in time. In addition, there is always an undercurrent flowing from public perception of the adequacy and fairness of policing and judiciary, and the representative biases of the legislature, that shift along party fault lines.

Laws bring order out of chaos

It is not the white line on the road that defines the flow of traffic. It is the system, of which the white line is symbolic of the need for order and control. The public agreement to accept the rules of the road makes complex, high speed, high volume traffic flow sustainable. The decision to drive on the left, or right, of the line was arbitrary, but everyone recognised the need for a single regulated system to avoid chaos.

The rules of the road minimise, among other things, the potential for the infliction of harm to others. The policing of the rules of the road, to ensure compliance, is necessary because some do not respect the rights of others not to be put at risk of harm.

Aviation authorities developed and enforce through licensing and inspection complex codes of control, and enforced maintenance standards. Flight paths and operational control frameworks maximise safety, but at a high cost. But the cost is accepted by the aviation industry and passengers as necessary to provide emotional comfort to passengers that they will not be harmed. They will be safe.

These types of rules fall into an easily definable class of laws and regulations to do with safety: including food, pharmaceuticals, health, sanitation and pollution. But law by itself is no deterrent.

> When men are pure, laws are useless; when men are corrupt, laws are broken.
>
> (Benjamin Disraeli)

Laws efficiently, effectively and justly enforced, provide a foundation for control.

> Government can easily exist without laws, but law cannot exist without government.
>
> (Bertrand Russell)

Good laws, badly enforced, create a culture of non-compliance that erodes public confidence and ultimately erodes the social fabric. Bad enforcement includes:

48   *The human animal*

- Corrupt enforcement where bribery can be used to avoid prosecution, minimise the punishment, or to direct prosecution against another;
- Non-enforcement (e.g. non-pursuit of the corrupt elite, or to stop tax evasion);
- Selective or discriminatory enforcement.

Better no law than laws not enforced.

(Italian proverb)

Bad laws, rigorously enforced, create a culture of repressed rebellion and resentment. A law is bad when:

- The premise on which it was based was wrong;
- The world has changed and the law is no longer appropriate;
- The law breaches fundamental principles of equality, fairness and non-discrimination;
- The cost of enforcement is greater than the damage being prevented;
- The complexity of the issue is such that it is not amenable to blunt legal control;
- The subject is one where laws should not be made – e.g. tastes and beliefs.

There is also the well-intentioned dilemma created when police and regulators take action against those who are behaving badly, but where there is no law sanctioning intervention. Police and regulators should not act without power, no matter how justifiable their actions, as this calls into question the integrity of the system. It subjects the regulator to court challenge and financial redress notwithstanding frustration and public opprobrium.

The parallel dilemma occurs when the police, legal and judicial systems are seen as ineffective and extra-judicial action is taken, exemplified by the killing of drug lords and traffickers under the direction of Rodrigo Duterte, the President of the Philippines.

Laws' temporal and geographic dilemmas

Law always lags developments in society – whether the developments are changes in values and beliefs, structural changes driven by growth, or advances in science and technology. It takes considerable time for an issue to first gain credence, then gather momentum and finally be enshrined in law. Rarely can an idea emerge and a law follow without following a time-consuming, demanding path, except perhaps in dictatorships or existential emergency. This delay is good, minimising gyrations in legality that would occur if laws simply enshrined temporary whims and fads. But delay has negative consequences.

Have you ever wondered:

- Why are there stupid, out-of-date laws still on the books?
- Why are there no laws, when something is crying out to be regulated?

How beliefs, religion, ethics and the law shape behaviour 49

- Why the law criminalises behaviours that should, in your opinion, not be criminal, and conversely, explicitly or implicitly, condones behaviours that should be criminalised?
- How at different times the same behaviour changes status from legal to illegal? How fair is it to those who were punished for breaking a law that has since been repealed? Should the conviction be quashed and the prisoner freed and restitution paid?

The following are examples of actions that are both legal and illegal, at the same time, but in different countries or jurisdictions within one country:

- Homosexuality;
- Abortion;
- Prostitution;
- Women driving a car;
- Alcohol possession and consumption;
- Women wearing bikinis or burkas.

The following are examples of actions that have changed from legal to illegal and vice versa simply by the passage of time:

- 'Hard' drugs such as opium and cocaine;
- Alcohol was legal, then made illegal and then re-legalised in the USA;
- Child labour;
- Slavery;
- Same sex marriages;
- Segregated transport, restaurants and public facilities.

While the time-lag in a change of the law helps to ensure that social evolution is more stable, the failure to enact laws in a timely fashion can have major consequences for social stability and cohesion.

Changes in laws caused by innovation, invention and our evolving world are understandable. 'We couldn't regulate what we didn't know or imagine', is a legitimate defence for lawmakers when justifying a new law or the failure of an old one. Nowhere is this more evident than in the world of finance, which has seen an explosion in product complexity beyond the understanding of all but a few *quants*. Both the corporations that sold the products and the regulators entrusted with policing their sale were ignorant of the products' real operations and the potential for catastrophe.

Changes in modes of transportation – the car, aeroplanes – and communication – radio, TV and the internet – profoundly impact human interaction. Those changes generate the need for regulation to protect individuals from exploitation and to avoid chaos and uncertainty. The law could not anticipate these developments, does not adequately regulate them in a timely manner and cannot anticipate what is yet to come.

50 *The human animal*

Laws will always lag change, but even once the change is identified, framers of laws rarely imagine future changes. Legislatures consistently fail to predict the impact of new technology, the concentration of commercial power or innovative financial products.

The internet is challenging many models of communication and commerce. Borderless supply and ephemeral sales-and-delivery channels impact tax liability and consumer protection. Twitter, Facebook, the Dark Web, Torrent file sharing and WikiLeaks continue to change how we view and exchange knowledge and intellectual property, privacy, and rights and liabilities. The law is slowly evolving to deal with these issues.

The explosion of commercial regulation during the twentieth century was a direct consequence of major crises and scandals. Raised public consciousness developed into public anger, which was vented on politicians, who wanted to be re-elected. Ultimately, self-interest generated sufficient political will to enact correcting laws and regulations, though not without resistance from those whose interests were threatened by the new laws.

Some organisations increased massively in size and in power, requiring laws that limited the kinds of competitive (or predatory) behaviours they could indulge in. A century of competition and anti-trust law evolved – but only after the fact.

Unfortunately, the promulgation of laws is not always for the common good. Often laws are changed, or not implemented, to satisfy a narrow sectional interest, or to assuage transient social values. When pressure is brought to bear on the legislature to legalise, or criminalise, a behaviour in the interests of a few (except where there is the rectification of unjust laws[8]), the foundation of the legal systems as a whole is called into question.

Globalisation and the pressure from diversity

The evolution of societies from discrete, relatively small, homogenous communities into an interconnected, yet highly diversified and complex globalised community has changed the way laws need to be framed and how they will be perceived. Except in the smallest communities, custom is not enough to regulate behaviour. The vast majority of us do not live in small, homogenous, devoutly mono-religious villages, where a single religion, supported by a clearly defined power hierarchy that exercises real control, provides a ruling force, independent of any legislative imperative.

We live in a globalised, pluralistic world without a single unifying force. Activities span national, legal and cultural boundaries. Crossing boundaries increases the potential for conflict between diverse beliefs and values.

A homogenous society, with a single religion-based values system, could be regulated by a one-size-fits-all approach. Rapid amendment to laws, reflecting changes in the environment, could readily be made to align with the single moral compass. A pluralist society, by contrast, may divide in opinion, making regulating change more difficult. The USA is a classic example of paralysis through political polarisation of secular doctrinal, though often religiously inspired, differences. The domination of the three arms of legislation by the Republican Party has created an environment where one set of beliefs may be enshrined in laws that conflict with at least half of the beliefs of the population. There is potential for legalised tyranny of the majority.

The issue of favouritism is not limited to race. Claims of bias include laws for the rich, for industry, for social welfare and for or against the environment. Competing vested interests claim and counter claim. The response of the legal system is clumsy. It is not selective. One size fits all. All laws apply to everyone equally within the jurisdiction.

Globalisation and mass migration have accelerated the fragmentation of social uniformity within individual nations. While diversity has incalculable benefits, it brings with it potential problems for behaviour, particularly where migrants bring with them widely divergent sets of values. The clash of value systems, compounded with tribalism, is the root of much inter-community conflict. It is harder to appeal to the civic mind when it is fragmented, and where the law is seen as biased, unjust and discriminatory.

This is not just a social issue, but a practical problem for businesses with a multi-cultural staff mix. The problem of difference and jurisdictional reach is magnified in the international commercial arena. Businesses must operate within systems of laws in multiple sovereign states, each of which has enshrined its particular values and interests in bodies of laws. Differing levels of maturity in legal systems and political stability exacerbate the problem for multi-nationals.

The expansion of trade from village-centric to regional, national and now global has changed requirements for product quality and commercial behaviour. Where once word of mouth, shaming and direct appeal to local authority would have limited a merchant's ability to sell shoddy produce, or mislead and deceive, now national and global laws and systems need to be put in place to regulate global merchants, especially those with residence in convenient jurisdictions.

Find the gap and the role of lawyers

The asynchronous development of laws in time, focus and priority is a major source of systemic legal differences, often resulting in a conflict of laws. This is a rich playground for corporations and high-net-worth individuals to arbitrage, to their advantage, the differences in laws on property, inheritance and tax.

It is generally accepted that the proper purpose of laws is to 'better' regulate society in order to protect the individuals within it. However, the law, as discussed earlier, is not perfect, being a time-lagged facsimile of social requirements. Changes in society, technology and commerce are more rapid than the laws designed to regulate them. Quite often the framers and enforcers of laws do not fully understand the nature of cutting edge advances and all the implications and potential damage that may flow. Corporations can afford to buy the best brains, outcompeting regulators and framers of legislation.

52   *The human animal*

The framing of laws is a complex task and is rarely comprehensive, let alone perfect. It would be impossible to document in law every nuance of possible behaviour. The interpretation of law is thus an art, not a precisely engineered construct.

While there are some laws that are prescriptive and precise, there is a great body of law that has been developed by judicial interpretation. The courts use principles and precedents to allow them to interpret laws and apply them in unforeseen contexts.

A key role of lawyers is to advise clients of the legality of actions. Few clients deliberately set out to flout the law. For those that do, this book is unlikely to be on their reading list.

One of the first steps in the commercialisation of an idea, or the launch of a new product, is to get an answer to the question:

1.   Is it legal?

The answers are not always a simple yes or no. If the answer is yes, it is legal, then that is the end of the primary investigation, but if the answer is 'Yes, subject to ...' or 'No! It is not legal', then the next questions typically are:

1.   What are the specific legal impediments?
2.   How do I get around the impediments? What gaps are there?
3.   What is the minimum needed to comply?

As fast as laws are devised, their evasion is contrived.

(German proverb)

Finding the gaps has become an art form in the world of tax planning. Avoiding tax is a crime. Minimising the exaction of tax through legal structures is a game of skill and daring. To some it is seen as a moral imperative, justified by the creeds of 'taxation is theft', or 'maximising shareholder return', or 'everyone is doing it'. Governments, influenced by lobbyists, party faithful and the prevailing political wind, open or close the deductibility and assessibility gaps. The role of the tax advisor is not simply to ensure compliance with the law, but also to introduce to their clients ideas for tax minimisation – an active strategy of finding the gaps.

Finding and exploiting gaps and loopholes is not restricted to tax law. If the legal universe was placed on a globe, you could spin it and, blindfolded, stop it at any point. The question could be asked: 'How can I get an advantage there by finding a gap in the law that restricts, or requires actions, that impact me unfavourably?'

The search for minimum legal compliance is exploited across jurisdictions and legal domains. Notorious areas for gap detecting include:

*   Taxation;
*   Environment;

How beliefs, religion, ethics and the law shape behaviour 53

- Urban Planning and Construction;
- Occupational Health and Safety;
- Competition (anti-cartel);
- Banking and Insurance;
- Corporate Liability;
- Insider compliance through porous Chinese walls.

The recent financial crisis evolved out of the exploitation of gaps in the regulatory globe. Why did these gaps exist? There are three broad causal themes:

- Gaps were created by the deliberate removal of prohibitions following the dictate of the ***market place morality mask***.[9]
- Gaps existed because of the absence of laws to cover new products and ***technical product packaging innovations***.[10]
- Gaps were created recognising that, while there were general principles[11] covering an activity, there were no specific legal prohibitions.

Finding and exploiting gaps is believed by many to be the duty of executives, to maximise shareholder value and, in turn, their own remuneration.

Unintended cultural consequences of the gap mindset

There is little doubt that exploiting gaps provides opportunities for profit. Depending on the nature of the gap, and the mindset of politicians, the gap may stay open for decades, far beyond the life expectancy of the average CEO's tenure, or that of politicians, or senior regulators. Short-term profit maximisation satisfies analysts, brokers and shareholders, who demand quarterly gains in wealth. It feeds the market beast, the most powerful of modern myths.

There are, however, negative consequences to the gap mindset. The most obvious is the issue of latent liability. Billions are paid in restitution, and even more in costs for changing corporate systems. Plus there is the headline cost of paying fines to regulators. The consequent destruction of trust, unfortunately, has no line in the balance sheet. Ultimately, the major impact of gap exploitation, once regulated or made public, is on the shareholders. The responsible executives will have claimed their bonuses and many will have moved on.

The monetary cost has been in the billions, but the real damage is to brands and trust, which will take decades to repair. Fear and anger and the loss of trust operate in the primitive part of the brain. Overcoming these negative beliefs cannot be done with PR spin or even with facts.

A third, more insidious, effect of the gap mindset is its impact on adherence to internal controls and influence on the corporate culture. Whether we like it or not, we emulate our leaders. They influence us to change our beliefs. The behaviours and tone at the top have more impact on staff behaviour than any written values or code of conduct. If leadership dictates that it is corporate policy to find gaps and shade the law, then staff will emulate looking for the

54 *The human animal*

gaps, in laws, contracts and agreements, and even in the internal codes and practices.

Conclusion

Laws are inadequate as a basis for setting global behaviour standards. They suffer from the same limitations as values and religions.

- Laws vary according to jurisdiction;
- They change over time.

The determination of right and wrong, good or bad, should not be dependent on where you happen to be, or when you ask the question.

Law also suffers from a structural fissure. There is a chasm. Not all illegal acts are harmful and not all legal acts are harm free. Being legal or illegal does not make an action right or wrong, which is why strict legal compliance by corporations will never rebuild trust while they continue to exploit gaps, defending their actions by donning a cloak of legality while ignoring the harm.

In the next chapter, we examine harm and the Harm Principles and determine to what degree they provide a universal framework to guide public and corporate behaviour and decision making in our complex globalised world.

Notes

1 James M. Buchanan, *The Limits Of Liberty: Between Anarchy and Leviathan.* Chicago: University of Chicago Press, 1977.
2 Aristotle, Plato and the Epicures applied incorrect scientific models to explain and justify philosophies of conduct and behaviour.
3 The splits in the Christian churches resulted in wars, repression and the Inquisition. Splits in Islam between Sunni and Shiite are the basis for sectarian wars that continue today.
4 From a diary, written in pencil by a British soldier and recovered from his body in a First World War trench.
5 Merriam-Webster's Dictionary of Law, © 1996 Merriam-Webster, Inc.
6 The Borg is a fictional cybernetic race from the Star Trek universe. The Borg absorbs other races and perfects them by injecting cybernetic components, subduing individual will to that of The Collective.
7 Chapter 1.
8 The Australian Constitution was amended to remove discrimination of Aboriginals in 1967.
9 Deregulation of the financial markets was a deliberate US policy.
10 There was limited understanding of the real balance sheet value of derivatives and insured instruments, allowing for an explosion of balance sheets.
11 Affordability had been a key plank in sound lending, as was selling appropriate products to meet customer needs.

3   The nature of trust

Key points

- Trust is a belief – a state of mind.
- Trust is independent of the values set. The essential ingredient is that the parties share values which they believe will be adhered to.
- The mechanism for trusting is a mixture of inherited biology, brain chemistry and cognitive processing and analysis of facts and experience.
- Removing fear of harm builds trust. Creating fear of harm destroys trust.
- Rebuilding trust requires an understanding of the power of fear, the nature of belief systems and how they impact on individual perception, understanding and behaviour.

Conclusion

- Trust is critical to social order and cohesion. It reduces friction and tension in relationships. Trust makes doing things with others easier.

For the corporation

- Trust is critical to corporate efficiency and effectiveness.
- Trust is an invisible asset that leverages performance.
- Rebuilding trust starts internally and radiates to customers, suppliers and the community.
- Creating a belief that the corporation will not inflict harm through any of its activities is the primal trust building block.
- Corporations that are believed to be actively reducing harms, not just of their own making, will build trust and engagement with staff and the community. This is a foundation for corporate social responsibility with which staff can truly identify. Reciprocal altruism is part of our DNA.

56 *The human animal*

3.1 The elements of trust

Trust is a belief. This belief may have logical and rational foundations, or simply spring from a leap of faith. Trusting is a state where we believe we understand the predictable intentions and actions of others, whether the others are people, organisations, animals, or animate or inanimate objects.

Trusting is an inherited survival mechanism. We needed to trust our own tribe and leaders if we wanted to survive. But we are not born to trust. Survival required that first we mistrust others. We feared others. It is what kept us safe. Stranger danger is still one of the earliest lessons parents teach their children. We are taught to be careful, suspicious and even fearful, especially of those who do not belong to our family, our tribe. Others!

Overcoming these fears requires cautious exposure and desensitisation. Trusting is thus an outcome that takes time to establish. We learn to trust, but are ever ready to fall back to the safety of mistrust when harmed or threatened with harm.

If something is feared it is unlikely to be trusted. The threat of harm triggers fear. Corporations that threaten harm will not be trusted. Conversely, corporations that reduce harm and engender safety will be trusted.

Unlike ethics, norms, religions, laws and even the Harm Principles, which profess to shape behaviour through dictates of what is right and wrong, trust operates at a visceral level which influences our feelings and behaviour. Trusting is not simply the product of logic, reason, fact and truth.

Understanding how trust is created, used and lost is difficult because trust is intangible, a belief, that is sometimes supported by facts and experience but often exists in spite of experience and facts.

Trust is not logical. It can be unfairly lost through baseless fear and rumour. It is most often destroyed by 'bad' behaviour. What follows is an exploration of how trust is given – from one party to another and taken away.

3.2 The value of trust

The importance of trust cannot be overestimated. It is difficult, if not impossible, to cooperate in an environment of distrust, whether at the personal, social, corporate, national or international level. While the following list references corporations, the principles apply to every relationship. Trusted corporations do more business with less cost.

Typically, inside a high trust corporate environment:

- Communication is more open and respectful.
- Differences are resolved with less emotion and less conflict.
- Decisions are made on solid criteria after robust analysis and discussion.
- The barriers between silos are more porous.
- There is a greater identity with the entity, rather than just the team.
- Ideas can be raised without fear.

The nature of trust   57

- Creativity and problem solving increases.
- Real collaboration and cooperation increases.
- Relationships are stronger and less superficial.
- Mistakes are managed without fear.
- Problems can be raised so that whistle-blowing can be managed internally without fear.
- Employee recruitment is easier and retention is greater.
- Overall effectiveness and efficiency increases, and
- Work is more enjoyable, with all the benefits that feeling good has on morale, health, satisfaction and engagement.

Where there is an internal culture of distrust:

- Decisions and activities are slower.
- Rules proliferate.
- Audit focus increases.
- Absenteeism and accidents increase.
- Whistle-blowers feel the need to go outside.
- The quality of work decreases.
- Employee disengagement increases,[1] and
- Staff resignations increase.[2]

When a corporation is trusted in the market place by investors, customers and suppliers perceptions of risk (fear) decline. Highly trusted corporations have:

- Lower cost of sales because there is less effort required to make a sale and keep a customer;
- More reliable and flexible relationships with suppliers;
- Better market performance;
- Less regulatory scrutiny;
- Greater media support (formal and social); and
- Greater support in difficult times – mistake forgiveness is possible.

The converse is true when the corporation is distrusted. Corporations that are distrusted have more difficulty raising capital, attracting staff, making sales and avoiding regulatory scrutiny. When things go wrong, the public enjoys the spectacle of the downfall. *Schadenfreude is alive and well.*

The concept of trust appears in a variety of publications dealing with behaviour in organizations and in institutional settings (e.g. Schein, 1969: Argyris, 1970; Fox, 1974). In general, the consensus of opinion is that trust between individuals and groups within an organization is a highly important ingredient in the long-term stability of the organization and the wellbeing of its members.[3]

58 *The human animal*

Trust is social and corporate oxygen. Without it relationships die. With it they flourish. Unlike oxygen, which can be scientifically analysed, measured, captured, stored and used at will, trust is ephemeral. We can empirically assess the role of oxygen in supporting life and growth. The role of trust is inferred.

Trust is a corporate asset, yet it has no line item in the balance sheet.

3.3 Trust and the market economy

Trust is a lubricant that facilitates interaction. Our entire financial system is built on trust, though some cynics would say faith. The idea that a piece of paper has monetary value beyond its negligible intrinsic value is the foundation of modern currencies. People believe that there is stored value in the paper, because they trust the government that issued it. Based on this trust we exchange real goods and services for paper-evidenced promises. In truth, except for times of financial crisis, most people are unaware of the complex beliefs in play in the use of money. It is so ingrained in the everyday that we have no fear of the idea that the paper is worthless.

Similarly, we take our money and give it to our banks. We do so hoping that the banks are trustworthy, believing that money deposited will be returned when asked for. We trust that the fees will be as disclosed, that the services will be as explained and the income on investments will be realised. Every financial crisis results in runs on the bank, where people who have lost trust in the banks want their money in cold hard cash, even if the cash is worthless, as happened in the Weimar Republic at the end of World War I. The prime focus of central banks in the Global Financial Crisis was to stabilise emotions, reducing fear that the banks would collapse.

The only thing we have to fear is fear itself.

(FD Roosevelt)

Electronic banking extends the dimension of trust to the security, integrity and trustworthiness of the computer systems and the internet. While cybercrime proliferates, it is kept as much as possible out of the public arena to minimise the loss of trust of the unsophisticated public in the electronic systems which allow banks to make huge cost savings and expand the range of products and scope of services.

Trust in money, banks and electronic banking is one of the fundamental engines of modern commerce. If trust was lost and we needed to revert to physical currency, or in the extreme, gold or barter, the international economy would be destroyed. When trust in a currency is lost, its ability to be used as a medium for exchange of value disappears. When a bank collapses, it causes distrust in all banks, threatening a contagion. The actions of central banks to

The nature of trust 59

stem the contagious growth of distrust enabled the banking system around the world to continue during the GFC.

The absence of positive trust introduces inhibiting frictions. At the extreme, where there is active distrust, having any kind of productive interaction is extremely difficult, if not impossible. The US–Iran relationship is one of mutual distrust. The same is true of Israelis and Palestinians. Distrust is a barrier that needs to be overcome before any positive outcomes are possible. Overcoming distrust takes resources and time. It is visceral and not always logical because it is founded in fear – our most fundamental primitive driver. Eliminating fear is not simple.

Having a trusted brand is the Holy Grail. Businesses invest heavily in building the brand and defending it from attack because having a trusted brand removes barriers to doing business. Customers of a trusted brand have little or no fear or angst. The company is freed to focus on satisfying customers' needs and wants, and positioning their products competitively instead of defending their position on the swampy foundation of fear and the threat of harm.

A trusted brand is not the same as brand awareness. Awareness is only recognition of existence – not whether the brand is trustworthy or not. Trust in a brand is the same as in personal relationships. There needs to be demonstrated delivery against the brand promise, either directly to each consumer or to those who influence their purchasing decisions such as their trusted peers, family or influencers (often star-powered celebrities) – leaders they trust to guide them.

Toyota, once heralded as the most reliable auto manufacturer, lost the trust of customers with a string of recalls that damaged sales. Volkswagen is undergoing a crisis of trust, not just as a corporation, but for the brands it owns because it lied to its customers about the level of harmful emissions generated by its vehicles. By contrast, Volvo built a brand around keeping occupants free from harm. Boring but safe. Trusted.

Catholic priests were once trusted but the Church failed to prevent harm to its members from abuse by the priests. Not only did it fail to act by punishing the offenders, it actively protected them, denying responsibility, covering up and resorting to legal manoeuvring to minimise restitution and remediation. The Church abused its power, using faith as a tool to suppress action and the law to suppress publication of settlements. These actions generated massive distrust, damaging the church's standing (brand) and power. The actions of the Church are not unique to religious institutions. We have witnessed these tactics, minus the element of faith, on numerous occasions in commercial, political and social corporations and governments.

Every time a corporation from any industry is exposed and fined for malpractice of one form or another, whether it is low product quality, poor labour relations, financial irregularity or poor service, brand value declines.

The closer the link between the product and individual perception of potential harm, the greater the impact of poor behaviour. For the Church, the link was as close as is possible. Priests not only breached trust, but they broke rules that they had imposed and, at a primitive level, abrogated their prime duty as leaders, to

60   *The human animal*

keep followers safe. Threatening the safety of our children breaches the primal directive – the survival of our DNA.

3.4 Building and earning trust

Building trust is a critical part of building relationships, in every society, regardless of size, structure, composition or purpose. Trust is the invisible glue that holds everything together. In business, trust is the lubricant that makes doing deals easier. The same is true in personal relationships, politics and international diplomacy, which is why Trump's erratic behaviour is so destabilising to allies and enemies alike. The unpredictability destroys trust.

Trust takes time to build. It requires the demonstrated, consistent, repeated performance of an expected, or promised, behaviour.

> Trust arrives on foot and leaves on a horse.
>
> (Dutch proverb)

Once trust is given, it often exposes the person giving the trust, because they now believe they are freed to spend less time being cautious. There is a vulnerability when relying on the behaviour of another person, animal or thing. NASA developed a food testing regime for suppliers. The HACCP-certified supplier could deliver goods to NASA without having to subject each delivery to expensive and time-consuming inwards inspection. Providing the supplier adhered to the 'trusted process', everything was fine. The risk for NASA was a systemic failure to adhere to the agreed standard of behaviour. The consequences for astronauts eating contaminated food were severe, hence the rigour put into establishing, proving and then monitoring adherence to the trusted standard.

There is a hierarchy in building trust:

- First-hand experience (self)

  - I trust the bridge won't fail because I have walked across it recently many times;

- Second-hand experience of trusted others (friends, peers, opinion makers, celebrities)

  - My best friend loves it …
  - Movie star xx uses it;

- Guarantee by a trusted entity (inspection agency)

  - (Drug and Food, Organic Association);

- Established and trusted brand

  - Apple's new product;

The nature of trust 61

- The novice promise (a leap of faith)

  ○ Apple's iPhone at launch.

Where the experience is first-hand, the trust is stronger. I trust that bridge will hold my weight because I have used it many times. I trust Bill because he has always behaved honestly and kept his promises. I trust this business because they have always delivered what was agreed and fixed problems properly.

If a trusted friend, or colleague, tells you that you can trust Bill, then the degree to which you will trust Bill will depend on the degree to which you trust the person giving the recommendation, and whether they have demonstrated the quality of this type of judgement or assessment previously. Trust by proxy is not as strong as trust built on personal experience.

> Starting with Ebay, rating systems have typically been described as a way of establishing trust between strangers. Some commentators go so far as to say ratings are more effective than government regulation. 'Uber and Airbnb are in fact some of the most regulated ecosystems in the world,' said Joshua Gans, an economist at the University of Toronto, at an FTC workshop earlier this year. Rather than a single certification before you can begin work, everyone is regulated constantly through a system of mutually assured judgment.
>
> (John Driezza)[4]

One of the best ways to build trust is to fix problems when they occur. Brand loyalty is not just built on product performance, but performance after something goes wrong.

Trust grows when there is a shared perception of commonly held values that will be acted on. It does not matter what the values are. Trust is indifferent to the specific values held. Violent gangs and terrorist groups have sets of values. They believe other members will adhere to those values and that those values will be enforced. We may despise the values held by gangs and terrorists but we cannot deny the level of trusting loyalty amongst its members.

In the corporate world, trust is built through a number of mechanisms. One of the most important is promise and performance. Apple is one of the most trusted companies. Apple marketing embodies extravagant promise, but also delivers extravagant products that in the main perform as promised.

VW built its reputation on delivering quality products that performed. The unfolding saga of deliberately misleading environmental testing agencies through clever software has destroyed much of the trust. The VW case is interesting on several levels. The obvious is the deceit, which destroys believability. The second, and more subtle, is the callous infliction of environmental harm through breaching emission limits.

A second builder of trust is the belief that the trustworthy will not harm you. VW has breached this. VW owners may not have been directly harmed by the

62   *The human animal*

emissions, but the collective common was. If VW lied about its green credentials, what else was it covering up?

Too often, slick marketing and communications campaigns are utilised as substitutes for the slow process of building trust, block by block. But employees, customers and the market are increasingly cynical of highly polished messaging full of claim and wonder.

3.5 Belief and faith-based trust

> Faith consists in believing what reason cannot.
>
> (Voltaire)

There is a continuum from empirical trust to faith-based trust.

There are those who use the word trust without any empirical basis, or persist in trusting in the face of a growing body of evidence. Steve Jobs trusted his pancreatic cancer treatment to a holistic approach. If he had accepted the more proven medical treatment, he might still be alive. His belief in an unproven approach diminished his chances of survival.

Faith-based trust stems from the perceived power of the particular divinity to protect believers from harm, or to grant favour.

For the non-believers, those who trust out of beliefs or faith are naive.

3.6 Destroying trust

Destroying trust is easy. At a personal level within a corporation, trust is destroyed by behaviours or an environment, where there is:

- Abuse;
- Arbitrary use of power and decision making;
- Bad news is hidden;
- Bullying;
- Blaming;
- Disempowering;
- Dishonesty;
- Disloyalty;
- Disrespect;
- Errors and mistakes are punished;
- Favouritism and bias;
- Impossible goals;
- Improper conduct;
- Lack of accountability;
- Lack of appreciation;
- Lack of freedom to decide and act;
- Lack of mutuality;
- Lack of truthfulness;

The nature of trust 63

- Micromanaging;
- Closed communications;
- Selfishness;
- Unreasonable demands and goals.

At a corporate level, trust-destroying behaviours include:

- Deceptive marketing;
- Poor products and services;
- Poor employee relations;
- Falsified earnings; and
- Regulator intervention.

The forgoing lists are by no means exhaustive, but what they have in common with other trust-destroying behaviours is that each behaviour will cause a degree of harm, or the threat of harm. Each behaviour generates a fear.

3.7 Rebuilding trust

If building trust is hard, rebuilding destroyed trust is harder because it takes time and a change in belief that the underlying fear-triggering harms have been eliminated and will not return. You need to get back to zero from minus zero before you can start to regrow positive trust.

Trust in the global financial system was destroyed in 2008. Banks and the finance industry were rated as the least trustworthy of international businesses.[5] (This untrustworthiness was not universal. In Egypt, banks and bankers were seen as a stabilising force during and after the Arab Spring.) Throughout the financial crisis, people still used banks, not because they trusted them, but because they had no choice. As we emerged from the crisis, fear of further loss (harm) was reduced by government intervention through bailouts and deposit guarantees. But has trust in banks and bankers since been rebuilt? Each time there is a fresh finance industry scandal, fear resurfaces and trust rebuilding again becomes necessary.

When Steve Jobs returned to Apple in 1987 after its near corporate death, he assiduously rebuilt a trustworthy profile, generating fanatical customer loyalty. Apple was not just harm-free, it was positively safer, easier and more reliable, even if more expensive. Not only would Apple never put you in harm's way, but the company was also cool.[6]

The airline industry is fanatical about safety, not because the number of people killed and injured in a crash is larger than road fatalities and injuries, but because the spectacle of a plane crash is so vivid it generates a lingering primordial existential fear. Fear generated by real damage is not as impactful as fear generated by perceived threat of harm. The mind plays games and magnifies the imagined. This is exploited in literature and in movies. It is why invisible threats such as radiation generate disproportionate fear.

64 *The human animal*

It was reported that in America more people[7] were injured on the roads after 9/11, when plane travel was restricted, than were injured or killed in the twin towers. Yet the fear, angst, horror and outrage is totally focussed on the death toll in the towers and the perception of an existential threat. According to the Center for Disease Control and Prevention, in 2013 there were 73,505 nonfatal firearm injuries and 11,208 homicides, many multiples of the deaths from 9/11. The question is, 'why is gun violence perceived as less harmful, notwithstanding the 372 mass shootings in 2015?'

It is only by understanding the psychology of fear and the link to threat, real or perceived, that leaders, particularly in the public arena and corporations, can develop messages to manage public reaction without compromising truth. Spin doctors have a tried and proven formula after a corporate incident to calm public perceptions: – apologise, reinforce how the accident was an aberration and against policy and values, promise a full investigation and make three promises: any faults will be fixed; the culpable will be appropriately dealt with; and it will never happen again. The loss of trust is minimised by diminishing the prospect of further harm. Importantly, there is less of a story for the media to pursue. The resignation of the VW CEO and the parade by the VW Board down the contrition catwalk are part of a well-established formula to stem the damage.

Building and rebuilding trust are not just about accentuating the positive. They are about removing fears of harm, which is why Apple moved so swiftly to diffuse the issue of employee working conditions in supplier factories.[8] Industries such as pharmaceuticals, food, transport and hospitality, where there is an inherent risk of direct harm to the consumer, invest in harm-perception management, even though that nomenclature is not used. Drug companies rely on regulatory approvals as a mark of their safety. Banks want you to feel safe when you deposit your money. Auto manufacturers and airlines stress safety features. Hotels seek high ratings for cleanliness and safety.

A plethora of 'trust me, I won't do harm' marques exist for the environment, wildlife, humane treatment, nutrition, heart disease and cancer. Celebrity endorsements have two levers to induce sales. The first is association – 'buy this and you will be like me'. The second is more subtle, 'you can buy this, I do, and you trust me, don't you! Don't leave home without it!'

What all these have in common is that they want consumers to feel safe.[9] While the marketers make safety a value, corporations rarely utilise the Harm Principles to shape their corporate values and culture. Imagine a work environment where safety and the reduction of harm were given a solid values-and-policy foundation.

3.8 The role of harm in building trust

Leaders who keep their followers feeling safe are trusted. A leader who can make followers believe that she will keep individuals and the tribe free from harm will be trusted. Unfortunately, the Harm Principles and the language of harm are not used in politics, in corporations or in common conversation.

Politicians talk in degrees of threat – from existential to financial. They use specific examples of harm such as famine, disease, disaster, drought, flood, civil unrest, invasion, death, destruction and loss of jobs, but never use the language of harm. They conjure up 'the others', who are ready to do us ill by taking our jobs, disrespecting our religion, culture and way of life, or threatening our public and personal safety. They are out there ready to do us harm. 'I will stop the harm!' The most recent beneficiary of this approach is Donald Trump. Whether he acts on his pre-election rhetoric, or not, it is clear he demonised, inflamed, highlighted fears, threats and losses, and promised solutions. Trust me! I'm not a politician!

Political leaders implicitly invoke harm in their promises, but the promises are expressed as positive actions, including job security, availability of medical treatment, crime prevention, international security and tolerance of difference. Social security provisions are about preventing harm through poverty. Spending on the military and police keeps us safe from foreign and domestic threats.

Politicians almost never use the word harm. The Harm Principles are not part of common language. It is not part of the academic or philosophical dialogue. It does not appear in religious language. The only place where harm linguistics is common is in legal[10] jurisprudence during the formulation of laws.

This is unfortunate because harm and the Harm Principles provide not only a readily accessible and understandable language but, most critically, they address the primal drivers of fear and safety and the link to building and retaining trust.

The language of harm is not used in corporate internal communications, or in external marketing. Harm does not appear in corporate values, not because harm is irrelevant, but because the idea of harm has never been fully considered and perhaps marketers and communications experts prefer positive language. Even researchers into the dynamics of trust express their results in positive language: *Leaders who keep their followers feeling safe are more trusted.*

Most values statements and their supporting materials fail to make the connection between how living the values reduces fear and harm and in so doing increases trust. To make matters worse, it is probable that these values statements will be reinterpreted according to local context and not in accordance with the intent of the board that approved them.

We operate in a globalised multicultural world. To get shared meaning and understanding requires a different linguistic. Harm provides the linguistic to achieve shared meaning and understanding, replacing the models which declare that certain values are good – because they just are. Harm provides a logical, more rational basis for determining 'goodness' while simultaneously addressing the deep psychological driver of fear of harm.

The greatest destroyer of trust is when expected values are not lived.

66 *The human animal*

3.9 Build trust by reducing harm

Great leaders build trust. People follow leaders who keep them free from harm or the threat of harm, or who will reduce the amount of harm being suffered by their national tribe. Thus, as a first step, leaders must identify those elements that could harm their followers and then make their followers believe they have the power and will to eliminate the offending elements.

Harm reduction to build trust works for business leaders and for corporations, reaching its apogee in politics. Political leaders need the trust of the people to be elected. Citizens trust political leaders who they feel will keep them safe and who will actively reduce the threat of harm. Citizens can be directly harmed by political leaders through:

- Graft and corruption;
- Promulgation of discriminatory laws;
- Discriminatory and arbitrary law enforcement;
- Misusing public finances for unnecessary programmes;
- Committing the country to an unnecessary war;
- Incompetence, etc.

There are three stages in the harm-trust cycle.

1. Identify and articulate the harms so those at risk believe you understand their problem.
2. Identify the harms that can be controlled and those that cannot.
3. Eliminate the harm and threat of harm, or promise how they will be reduced.

Doing it is not enough. Your staff, or the voting public, need to believe, and belief, as discussed earlier, is not about truth, facts and logic. All the factors discussed in Chapters 1 and 2 need to be considered in the design and execution of the communications approach.

Where does 'fake news' fit? Perpetrators of lies intentionally mislead the public in order to shape beliefs and, as discussed, beliefs are not influenced by simple refutation of the lies.

Labelling truth as 'fake news' is an attempt to delegitimise the source of truth that attempts to alert the public to the lies

3.10 Conclusion

Believing solely in the rational, logical, knowledge- and rule-based cerebral man as the primary force for civilising behaviour dooms us to repeat the failures of the past. Doing so makes us vulnerable to manipulation by those who prey on our inherited primitive survival drivers, promising to keep us from harm. Manipulators know that once their followers believe and trust, truth alone will be powerless.

Notes

1 Deloitte assessed the cost of disengaged employees to the economy at $300 billion annually. www2.deloitte.com/insights/us/en/deloitte-review/issue-16/employee-engagement-strategies.html.
2 Kenexa surveys have identified that 50% of staff who distrusted their leaders planned to leave.
3 John Cook and Toby Wall MRC Social and Applied Psychology Unit, University of Sheffield.
4 www.theverge.com/. . ./rating-system-on-demand-economy-uber-olive-garden.
5 Edelman Trust Barometer, /www.edelman.com/trust-barometer.
6 It would be interesting to conduct a survey of the harm index of corporations.
7 Professor Gerd Gigerenzer, a German academic specialising in risk, has estimated that an extra 1,595 Americans died in car accidents in the year after the attacks – indirect victims of 9/11.
8 The harm to employees of suppliers has become a major issue impacting the clothing and footwear industries.
9 If you Google 'Safety in Corporate Values', you will have over 7 million results.
10 Harm prevention is central to the reasoning in the creation of laws, but is rarely used in the broader public conversation about law. Post promulgation, the underlying harm is replaced with the specific criminalised actions.

Part II

Harm

But words are things, and a small drop of ink,
Falling, like dew, upon a thought produces
That which makes thousands, perhaps millions think.
— George Gordon Byron

4 Harms

Key Points

- There are two types of harm – physical and psychological.
- Harm can be inflicted on people, animals, property and the Common.
- Harm is a universal, applying equally regardless of race, religion, gender, age, sexual orientation or geography.
- Harm cannot be inflicted on ideas, beliefs and religions.
- There are many actions we do not like, or find uncomfortable, but which are not harmful.
- Societies use the threat and actual infliction of harm (punishment) to maintain social order. When the harm inflicted (a) is proportional to the criminal act AND; (b) where the harm inflicted is to prevent a greater harm; then the punishment is justified by the Harm Principles.
- Religious beliefs are used to justify the righteous infliction of harm. These actions offend the Harm Principles.

Conclusion

- Unlike beliefs, faith, ethics and laws, harm is an easily understood universal constant that applies equally, regardless of time and geography.
- Harm is immune from distortions inherent in cultural, philosophical, religious or legal differences.
- Thus, harm and the Harm Principles could be used in resolving conflicts of judgement and assessment in our globalised world.

For the corporation

- Harm is an easy concept for staff to understand.
- Harm resonates with our inherited behavioural drivers.

> • It is easier for staff in different situations and from different back-
> grounds to align with preventing individuals and their corporation
> doing harm than to be motivated by codes based on corporate defini-
> tions of what is right and wrong.

Once harm has been done, even a fool understands it.

(Homer (800 BC – 700 BC))[1]

If Homer is correct, then harm, unlike moral philosophy, or law, requires little in
the way of intelligence or learning to be recognised and understood. Appreciating
the meaning and impact of harm does not require holding any particular religious
beliefs, ascribing to a suite of philosophical constructs, or knowledge of principles of jurisprudence or laws.

The language of harm and the Harm Principles are elegant because they are:

- **Simple**, being readily understood, to the point of being self-evident;
- **Independent** of any particular set of values, moral or religious precepts or
  laws;
- **Neutral**, applying equally to everyone, transcending national, cultural,
  religious and legal boundaries;
- **Aligned** with religious precepts, cultural norms, codes of conduct and laws
  that govern behaviour;
- **Personal**, by addressing our most primitive survival drivers. Individuals can
  relate directly to and internalise the impact of harms.

The language of harm and the Harm Principles are a unifying model for
understanding and establishing behavioural norms for increasingly connected
societies in our globalised world. For corporations, the Harm Principles provide
a simple model that all staff, at all levels, can understand, support and apply in
guiding their actions and decisions.

In this chapter, we examine the nature of harm and the Harm Principles and
how they relate to the current models of guiding and assessing the correctness of
behaviour. In Chapter 4, we explore trust and the role of harm prevention in
building trust. In Chapter 5, the Harm Principles are applied to corporations. The
application of the Harm Principles in society is the subject of a companion
publication, due for release in late 2017.

Why bother?

The world needs a universally applicable way of guiding and judging behaviour. In Chapter 2, we identified why religions, beliefs, ethics, moral philosophy, values and laws are incapable of being used as a foundation to guide
behaviour in a globalised world. Each of the traditional systems is contextually

dependent. The rightness and wrongness of the same action change, dependent on geography and point in time. The legal system is gap-ridden. Laws arrive too late to prevent damage and rarely provide timely and cost-effective remediation and prevention. The very nature of legal systems spawned the art of finding and exploiting gaps in laws, with an unintended negative impact on culture and trustworthiness. Simply complying with the law is a minimum standard for corporations, but it is not enough to generate the goodwill and trust of clients, customers and employees.

Using the traditional models makes it difficult, if not impossible, for corporations, operating across national boundaries and cultures, to achieve a consistent, corporation-wide set of behaviours, notwithstanding vast investments in communication, training and compliance.

In Chapters 10 and 11 we will see how using the universal language of harm and the Harm Principles simplifies the process for corporations, making it easier for good people to understand what is required, and for the harmful actions of the not-so-good to be seen and exposed for what they are.

This chapter examines:

1. The types of harms;
2. Inflicting harm;
3. Measuring the degree of harm;
4. The Harm Principles; and
5. The relationship of the Harm Principles to religions, philosophy and the law.

4.1 The nature of harms

There are three primary types of harm:

*   Physical harm to people;
*   Psychological harm to people; and
*   Harm to property (including harm to the Common).

The Harm Principles are a self-contained set of neutral, non-judgemental constructs to facilitate the determination of right or wrong, good or evil. It is necessary to remove from the definition of harm and the Harm Principles any self-entrenched judgements implicit in the language of immorality to avoid contextual bias and circular argument. Dictionary definitions of harm often include concepts of immorality, evil or wrongdoing.

In framing what constitutes a harm for the Harm Principles, current ideas of bad, wrong or evil must be excluded to avoid contamination from context. Removing any implicit judgements enables a logical discussion about harm, the Harm Principles and how they can be applied to all situations.

In the 3,000 years of social and commercial evolution since Homer, mankind has developed new ways to inflict harm, and increased the scale of harm caused, but nothing about the nature of harm has changed. Today, as in Homer's world, harm is

74   *Harm*

experienced to our person in two dimensions – physical and psychological. While the type and range of property have changed, harm from the destruction, theft or deprivation of property has not, whether the property is owned by a person, a collective, an incorporated entity, the state, the public, or the Common.

4.2 Physical harm to people

Physical harm to people is such a simple, self-evident concept that it is examined only briefly to ensure completeness. Because physical harms to the person are visible, they are classified in legal literature as objective harms. They do not require interpretation by the observer.

There are many ways physical harm can be inflicted. There are overt physical acts such as being cut, maimed, burnt, drowned, raped, tortured and starved. The link between the action and the harm is clear. While science has increased the complexity of the instruments of harm, the lay person can still readily comprehend the physical harm caused by biological, chemical and radioactive agents – even if understanding the mechanism of the harmful agent is beyond them. They can make the link between cause and effect.

Physical harm does not discriminate according to race, religion, sex, age, nationality or sexual orientation. If a healthy hand is cut off, the physical damage or harm is the same regardless of who you are or where you may be. The same applies to killing. Dead is dead.

Harm does not attach to the instrument, but the outcome. A needle may prick the skin during the administration of medicine, causing temporary pain and damage to the skin and tissue. The same needle could destroy the function of an eye. A knife may inflict a superficial cut, be used in life-saving surgery or cause death through severing an artery or piercing a vital organ. A car is not an instrument of harm but can inflict harm. A gun is designed to harm, but may be the instrument of preventing harm. The instruments are neutral. It is how they are used that may or may not make them harmful.

Similarly, not all physical harms are equal. The quantum of harm has a dynamic range that is explored later. Understanding the quantum of harm is an essential element of the Harm Principles, particularly in situations of conflicts of harms, where choices need to be made between courses of action, all of which are inherently harmful.

4.3 Psychological harm

Psychological harm[2] is more difficult to identify and quantify than physical harm to people and property because the psychological damage is invisible. These 'invisible' harms in legal literature are referred to as subjective harms because the degree of harm perceived by observers is coloured by the observer.

> Mock trial jurors are more punitive when emotional harm to the victim is more severe. Specifically, mock jurors imposed more punishment on a

robbery defendant when the victim had a difficult time coping emotionally with the crime, compared to when the victim's emotional reaction was mild.

(Janice Nadler, Mary Rose)[3]

The imprecision does not disqualify psychological harm from being included as a harm that can be inflicted on people; it just reduces the certainty of whether there was harm or just a non-harmful emotional response. Psychologists and psychiatrists have catalogued triggers and outcomes but do not fully understand the mechanisms by which psychological damage is inflicted and repaired. There are disagreements on diagnosis, treatment, prognosis and even language. There are ill-defined issues of the immediacy of cause and effect, latency, severity and persistence of conditions. They do not understand why the same event will have different impacts on different people.

This professional divergence does not stop members of the public from using psychological terms in conversation, literature and in the media, with a degree of certainty that professionals would not claim. For example, the words stress and distress are commonly used but poorly understood. Is the person stressed to incapacity, or just feeling pressured and uncomfortable, or stressed in a way that stimulates performance? Human emotional response is nuanced and spans a wide dynamic range with imprecise intervals. Where is the transition from concern, to panic, to terror, to traumatised? from upset, to despair? from being startled, to being morbidly paralysed by fear?

This section illustrates the difficulty in assessing the precise point at which a psychological reaction is harmful and the quantum of the harm being inflicted. This poses a practical dilemma that will be discussed later when considering individual responses and why being upset or offended is not a harm.

4.4 Harm to property

Property has a broad meaning, including goods, chattels, land, structures or conceptual assets such as ideas and inventions. Property can be physical, like land, animals, possessions and currency; or intangible like reputation and brand; or legal constructs like shares, financial deposits, investment in financial instruments; or rights over ideas and creations expressed as copyright and intellectual property. Property can have extrinsic value determined by what others will pay. It may also have intrinsic value that only the owner fully appreciates, such as a memento or family heirloom with negligible market value.

Harm to property can occur in many ways such as theft, destruction, damage and deprivation of access or use. As with physical harm to the person, harm to property is readily observable.

Because there are markets for the purchase and sale of property, assessing the quantum of harm is relatively straightforward, except for property with no market value but with high sentimental intrinsic value peculiar to the owner.

Unfortunately, in our complex world, nothing is simple, and harm to property does have gaps. If a car is 'borrowed' and returned washed, polished, repaired

76 *Harm*

and with a full tank of fuel, what is the harm if the owner was unaware? There was a legal trespass, even a transitory theft, but was there real harm to property, as distinct from the owner being upset? What if the owner was completely oblivious of the unauthorised use?

Is exposing the property to risk of damage harmful to the property, or is it just a question of the impact on the mental state of the owner? If the owner was blissfully unaware of the risk, what then? These and other subtle issues are dealt with later but do not diminish harm as a valuable construct to guide behaviour.

4.5 Universality

Unlike ideas of right and wrong, good or bad, legal or illegal, which developed from roots in different religions, local cultures or local laws, harm is non-discriminatory. Harm can be inflicted equally on all physical entities such as people, animals, property and the Common and on non-physical constructs such as corporations, societies and nations, regardless of identity or social difference.

The Harm Principles are universal because they apply the same way regardless of any unique or differentiating characteristics of the individual, or the time, or the location of the action. For example, if a knife is used to stab someone, then the primary harm inflicted will be the same regardless of race, religion, age, sex, nationality or geography, or whether it occurred today or last century, in New York, Moscow or Antarctica.

A critical distinction that must be made is the separation of the nature of harm itself from whether inflicting the harm is deemed acceptable or justified. There are many harmful acts, such as slavery, that were inflicted legally and with moral certainty. Who could be enslaved was determined by differences in race and religion. Law, custom and religion legitimised the discriminatory infliction of harm. Unfortunately, slavery is only one of many examples of the legitimisation of the discriminatory infliction of harm. As discussed previously, the fact that laws, religions and cultures selectively discriminate invalidates them as a universal guide for behaviour in our globalised world.

4.6 Harm to the common

Can property without an identifiable owner be harmed? Protection from harm of private property and state-owned property is clear, but what about items in our world that do not fall within state jurisdiction, such as oceans and the atmosphere, or because of their nature fall within state jurisdictions only while they transit the state's territory, such as air, water and migratory animals like birds and whales. The unowned have become known as the Common.[4] The Common is a form of property, which is not owned by an individual, corporation or state. The Common is owned non-exclusively by everyone in indivisible and unalienable shares.

The plurality of ownership does not diminish the ability of the Common to be harmed; it simply complicates who can use and defend the Common. The transient nature complicates the determination of who has jurisdiction to make laws to control use and protection.

The lack of legal status and ownership is further complicated by our lack of understanding of the mega systems involved. The full extent of harm to the Common may not materialise for several generations. The complexity of issues surrounding the Common does not mean it cannot be harmed. The Common can be harmed; we just do not have systems and structures to prevent the harm occurring or to prosecute those who have inflicted harm. The closest we get are international treaties, the effectiveness of which are limited by conflicting national interests.

Protection of the Common that falls within one nation is simple. The country declares a national park or marine zone. For endangered species, protection is by treaty, though not universally adopted and enforced. Rhino horn and ivory, for example, are relatively openly traded even in signatory countries.

Trans-national harms to air and water through pollution are complex. The source of harm may be in one country, but the harmful effects may be felt by neighbours and beyond. Countries regulate pollution to safeguard their national interests, not necessarily to be good neighbours. This is the essence of the climate change debate. Nations do not want to relinquish power and control by signing a treaty that may harm their domestic economy.

The local tribal interest outweighs the potential threat to a less immediate tribe. The failure to reach agreement on climate change is an example where conflicts of national interests safeguarding the present outweigh the potential collective harms to the future. Nations at different stages of development argue to protect their immediate self-interest where there is insufficient reciprocal benefit or threat of harm.

The rhetoric around climate change often devolves to right and wrong, which, as explored earlier, has no meaning in a cross-cultural discussion. Wrongs and rights, duties and obligations require leaps into the moral abyss when used to discuss behaviours around protection of the Common.

The Harm Principles need no such leap.

It would be possible to quantify harms already inflicted, harms that could be inflicted and the costs of the harm. This, however, is a politically naïve approach. After all, who could enforce a debt for past harms?

4.7 Incitement to harm

Inciting others to do harm is harmful. Even though the harm is indirect, there is a causal link between the incitement and the harm. It is the bullet that kills, but the finger that pulls the trigger. Incitement pulls harmful behavioural triggers. Often the link between incitement and harm is clear – a speech or a publication can be causally linked. But what happens when incitement arouses action, but the action is stopped? What happens if the incitement fails to arouse because the audience was unresponsive? Is the author of an article on a website that incites unknown readers to do harm culpable?

78   *Harm*

Inciting harm is in a similar category to ordering subordinates to do harm. With subordinates, there is structured power and control, often with consequences for failing to follow orders. With incitement, the source of the power differs. Power to incite derives from personal charisma or oratory, or is formalised institutionally in gangs and cults. Charismatic cult, gang or mob leaders incite followers to action by playing on visceral fears and prejudices that flow from strongly held beliefs that trigger our survival legacy drivers of fear of others, brain chemistry and the need to belong. The absence of a formal command-and-control structure does not negate the cause and effect. That members may have had a choice does not diminish the culpability of the inciting act.

There is a fundamental difference between being strongly critical of an idea or religion and inciting attacks on those who follow the idea or religion. While it may be painful or uncomfortable, even upsetting, for proponents of the idea, or adherents of beliefs or faiths, to have the object of their faith attacked, they are not harmed by the attack. They may be offended, dismayed or outraged but not harmed.

Criticism and disagreement are not harms. They can be beneficial. Challenging ideas and shibboleths is the basis of social and scientific evolution and has been instrumental in changing ideas such as the right to own slaves, the concept that the world is flat, the idea that witches should be burned, the concept that political power should be inherited or the idea that governments cannot be criticised.

4.8 The quantum of harm

The human capacity for inflicting harm

Our species has an unusual capacity for harmful action. Human traits include killing, maiming, exploiting, stealing, deceiving, humiliating, behaving recklessly, acting negligently or simply responding with cold indifference to the plight of others. Hereditary biology suggests that these selfish behaviours have their origin in the need to maximise the opportunity to pass on our DNA and to protect ourselves from perceived or real threats from others and eliminate competition. Regardless of the cause, these behaviours increase the threat of harm to the individual and to society at large.

Scientific advances have increased our ability to do harm. We have evolved from using spears, clubs, sabres and single-shot rifles to automatic high-powered weapons of immense range and lethal projection. Cannons, planes, rockets and now drones have extended our physical reach. We can project harm across continents, and the concept of identifiable, *legitimate* battlefields has all but disappeared.

The potential harms from technological advances are not limited to the military. Globalisation and the interconnectedness of economies through communications, trade and commerce have created single mega-system financial markets. A bad idea in one country can be harmfully exploited in all. Social media allows harms to be inflicted en masse, at a distance, in ways never conceived when the primary media of communications were limited in scope. Oral messages reached the immediate audience. Their dissemination required personal retelling, which often introduced distortions and embellishments. Physical publications such as pamphlets, newspapers and books were relatively costly and had limited distribution. It was not until we had broadcasts on radio and television that masses could be reached, but even these media were tightly controlled and access was restricted by ownership and legislative restrictions.

Now there is no such limit. With a smartphone and 140 characters, a worldwide audience can be reached. Each advance in technology expands the exercise of our rights and freedoms, but it is only in retrospect that we develop controls to mitigate the harms that may be inflicted.

4.9 Severity of the harm

Below is a non-exhaustive list of physical actions, set out in a rough hierarchy, to illustrate the continuum of severity. They are ranked from non-harmful to harmful. Where would you draw the line demarking those at the top as not harmful and those below as harmful?

- Look;
- Look with menace (leer, snarl ...);
- Touch (handshake);
- Pinch;
- Prick with a needle;
- Touch (sexual assault);
- Cut;
- Maim;
- Rape;
- Kill.

Depending on who you are, where you are, each of these actions may be perceived as being harmful. In devout religions, looking at a woman's hair is bad, but is it harmful? Similarly, any touching, even a handshake, may in some situations be a breach of a religious rule, distasteful and even offensive, but is it harmful?

At the other end of the spectrum, there is no ambiguity. Cutting, maiming, raping and killing are all unambiguously harmful, but may be legitimised by custom or law.

A rule of thumb for determining where to place the line could be that actions which are transient and do not infringe on the body of the person, even though they may be deemed improper by a culture or belief system, are not harmful. However, disrespecting beliefs and traditions, while not harmful, is insensitive, possibly inflammatory, and when done in a world where power can be wielded to protect beliefs from attack, dangerous, not because the act was harmful, but because those with power may inflict harm to protect their faith.

80 *Harm*

4.10 Persistence of the harm

The quantum of harm is also a function of how long it persists. A cut will heal, but an amputation will not. A short-term fright will fade, but a traumatic shock may persist over time and never disappear. The physical damage from rape may heal, but the psychological damage may last forever. A house may be destroyed, but can be rebuilt in time. Possessions can be replaced, but not those imbued with intrinsic value.

In harm to the Common, various kinds of wastes have different levels of persistence and hence produce different degrees of harm. Some harms to the Common will impact future generations, whether through degradation and pollution or through consumption of non-renewable resources. Protection of harm to the Common is difficult even for current generations. How can one prevent harm to future generations, who, not being born, have no legal status, or voice?

4.11 Actions at the edge of harm

Differences of taste, sensibility and faith generate a minefield of potential upsets. These upsets are not harms. Some people are deeply upset over different aesthetic styles such as art, dress, music and architecture. Some people love raw foods. Some eat things others find disgusting such as cockroaches, insects, monkey brains or whale. None of these emotional responses are harms.

Including upset or offense as a harm would allow people to set up mutable taste-based proscriptions on the behaviours of others.

Religious proscriptions on immodest dress, showing hair, diet, touching and extra-marital sex are examples in a similar category to taste and have no place in the pantheon of harms. They are belief-based and not subject to any form of rational analysis. Apart from the religiously inspired belief about the wrongness of the action, the action itself has no inherent harm. It is only wrong for the believer.

Dietary restrictions provide an interesting illustration. Janes do not eat any animal product, or root vegetables grown in the earth, where the cultivation may have damaged or killed animal life. Buddhists eschew eating animals, but have no qualms about eating root vegetables. Muslims and Jews eschew pork, but can eat the meat of cows, which the Hindus hold sacred. The prescriptions for halal and kosher are close, but are mutually disrespected.

There is no advantage in cataloguing all belief-based prohibitions. This very short set of belief-based non-harms is included to illustrate the point and to provide a heuristic to assist in the separation of belief/cultural/taste-based proscriptions and universal harms.

The exclusion of religious-based proscriptions is clouded because religions share many core proscriptions that are also harms. Almost all religions condemn murder, assault and theft. The problem is that each has different approaches to when killing is not murder, assault is punishment and the appropriation of property is compensation for insult. Most religions encourage charity, but some limit who should be the beneficiary. It is not that religious proscriptions *per se* are invalid; it is that they are founded on divergent belief systems and thus are of no value as a source for universal behavioural principles.

Most religious texts do not actively incite hatred and condemnation of other religions and their followers, but this has never stopped sectarian warfare in the name of defending the religion, or sect of the same religion, against other sects.

4.12 Susceptibility

Physical, sociological and cultural differences may influence the impact of the same action on different individuals. Being stabbed in the thigh will cause the same physical damage to anyone stabbed, but individual responses will vary. Special Forces, or highly-motivated warriors, have an emotional and physical toughness that makes them less susceptible to the impact of harmful actions. They might shrug off a stab that would incapacitate others. They suffer less from firefight-triggered stress disorders than ordinary soldiers and civilians.

At the other end of the spectrum, there are those with very low tolerances for pain or stressful situations. In the famous Egg Shell Skull Case, the harm caused was exacerbated because the victim had an abnormally thin skull. The aggressor could not rely on the unusual vulnerability of the victim as a defence in mitigation of the real harm inflicted.

Emotional responses differ markedly. Some cultures promote stoicism, acceptance of disagreement and criticism, while others indulge in public wailing, displays of emotion and are easily offended and angered. Where one society may feel deep discomfort, but tolerate the insult, others rise up to revenge the insult, particularly where there is a transgression of devout, usually conservative, beliefs.

While the holder of the beliefs may be demonstrably upset, there is no harm. Feeling upset is a choice flowing from a decision to believe. The demarcation from emotional upset to harm occurs when there is recognisable, persistent psychological damage.

Individual differences in susceptibility do not turn a non-harm into a harm and vice versa.

Notes

1 Homer, *The Iliad*, translated by Robert Fagles and Frédéric Mugler, with Introduction & Notes by Bernard Knox. Penguin, 1999.
2 The concept of psychological harm can also be extended to animals.
3 Janice Nadler and Mary Rose, Victim Impact Testimony and the Psychology of Punishment. *Cornell Law Review*, vol. 88:2 (2003).
4 The term common is used here to mean property, including air, water and land that may or not be owned, except perhaps by governmental agencies. The word common is used instead of the word environment. The Common includes the environment and also natural resources that may not commonly be perceived as being part of the environment. Environmental damage is subsumed within harm to the Common.

5 The harm principles

There is nothing new under the sun. Everything new is old.

(Proverb)

There are six Harm Principles. The underlying ideas embodied in the principles have appeared in different religious, ethical and legal forms, but have never been set out in the simple, universally applicable and understandable language of harms. The principles are:

1. Do no harm;
2. Freedom from harm;
3. Harming in self-defence;
4. Proportionality in harming in self-defence;
5. Balance of harms;
6. Prevent and reduce harms.

The first five principles are direct, covering relationships of two or more connected parties. The sixth principle is different and introduces an obligation to assist strangers.

Principle 1: do no harm

The founding principle, enunciated by Hippocrates, was:

First, do no harm.

Hippocrates' injunction was directed to the practice of medicine. It was created in a time when medicine was an art, rather than a science, where knowledge was limited and medical practice was as much folk lore as guesswork. If you don't know how to cure, at least don't make the problem worse. What makes his principle so profound is that he developed it in an era where harming others was the accepted norm.[1]

This elegant principle is the foundation of modern medical practice. It is as valid today as it was then. What is being proposed here is that it should be extended as a foundation for a universal code of conduct.

There is no reason why the injunction against the infliction of harm should be limited to medicine. As an absolute proscription, it is both simple and sophisticated. It is simple to understand. It is sophisticated because it can be applied to every kind of human behaviour and endeavour. It is a universal that transcends all geographic, ethnic and cultural boundaries. It is timeless. 'Do no harm' can be applied to our current view of the world. It can be used to interpret history and equally to regulate what we might do in the unimaginable future.

Do no harm is a positive obligation, or duty, requiring that actions do not inflict harm. The duty not to harm forms the underlying rationale of many laws and religious commandments (do not murder, steal, injure). It is also implied in many business principles and codes of conduct which enumerate specific harmful actions. The problem with enumerated proscriptions created to address specific conditions at a point in time is that every list will always have gaps. The more specific the items on the list, the greater the opportunity to parse meaning and for gaps to be found and exploited. Specificity, the province of lawyers, fails to accommodate complexity and changes wrought by the rapid and unforeseeable evolution of society and technology.

The injunction *do no harm* has no gaps and applies regardless of changes in society, technology or complexity. Imagine if every employee had a mindset that when doing their job, when being productive and achieving goals, they had as an overarching guiding principle – *first, do no harm*. It provides a unifying principle that can permeate every part of the corporation. It is equally applicable in the boardroom and the mailroom. It is fundamental to marketing, sales and product development. It can be applied in every jurisdiction and across borders.

The application of the first principle to corporate behaviour, values, culture and compliance programmes is explored in Part 3: Harm and The Corporation.

Principle 2: freedom from harm

The second principle embodies three rights:

- Each person has a right not to be harmed.[2]
- Each person has a right for their property not to be harmed.
- The Common has a right not to be harmed.

The first principle is a duty requiring that actions be free from harm. The second principle, is the reciprocal, involving the transposition from the doer of the action, to the recipient of the action. If the first principle is 'I must not harm' then the second principle is 'I have a right to not be harmed.'

The second principle is necessary because not everyone will adhere to the first principle. If no-one did harm, deliberately or inadvertently, there would be no

84 *Harm*

need for the second and subsequent principles. The reality is people will inflict harm. To stop them we need to be able to rely on a right to be free from harm.

Being free from harm or the threat of harm is part of our survival psyche. We look to our tribe and to our leaders to keep us safe. One of the principal duties of leaders is to keep followers safe. Feeling safe is one of the foundations for building trust and is essential for building and maintaining relationships, productive societies and commerce.

Inside corporations, employees want to feel that they will not be harmed by the corporation, bosses and fellow employees. Customers want to feel they will not be harmed by the corporation's behaviours, products and services.

Freedom from harm is one of the essential building blocks of civil society.

Principle 3: harm in self-defence

Notwithstanding the injunction not to inflict harm, there are individuals, collectives, corporations and nations who will endeavour to inflict harm in pursuit of their own interests, or because they simply enjoy or feel entitled to inflict harm.

Self-defence to prevent harm to yourself may require a breach of the first principle – do no harm. The first principle does not require pacifism and turning the other cheek. There is no logical reason to simply stand submissively waiting for harm to be inflicted by those who ignore the first principle. This is against the instinct to survive.

When there is a real threat of harm, it is totally appropriate to inflict harm to prevent harm to one's self and/or property, and, by extension, to the defence of third parties and their property (and to protect the Common).

The right to inflict harm in self-defence does not sanction inflicting harm in response to non-harmful actions, or to defend things which cannot be harmed. For example, if I feel insulted or offended this is not a harm. If I break a religious law, which beyond the narrow confines of the religion is not a harm, then I am not harming, and thus inflicting harm in self-defence cannot be invoked. I cannot harm you because you are verbally attacking my taste, personal preference or beliefs no matter how hurt I may feel.

Provided you do not harm me, threaten to harm me or incite others to harm me, there is no justification for me harming you, claiming *'harm in self-defence'*. The Harm Principles cannot be applied to justify harmful actions in defence of religions, beliefs and ideas or to assuage hurt feelings, no matter how intensely held.

Revenge, in response to a harm already inflicted, is not covered by the harm in self-defence principle. Self-defence is about prevention of harm. Revenge is about punishment and/or compensation. The judicial imposition of penalties as part of a punishment regime is in part justified by the self-defence principle when the harm inflicted as part of the punishment is to act as a deterrent, preventing future harms. In calculating the punishment of offenders, courts examine not only the harm inflicted by the offender, but also the value of the punishment as a deterrent to reduce future harm, not just by the particular offender, but as a warning to the public at large.

Principle 4: proportional harm in self-defence

When inflicting harm in self-defence the amount of harm inflicted should be proportional to the threat or harm being defended against. Being attacked by a feather does not justify defending with a howitzer. The concept is well entrenched in legal jurisprudence, but not always applied.

Normally, self-defence involves urgency. There is an imminent threat of harm. This lack of preplanning of self-defence provides some leeway in assessing proportionality. How much leeway will depend on the specific circumstances.

There are situations, such as in battered wives' syndrome, where there is the on-going infliction of harm. The perpetrator normally has an imbalance of psychological, physical or financial power. The premeditated killing of the perpetrator by the victim receives uneven treatment in the courts. The same difficulties face an analysis of whether the harm in self-defence was proportional. There is no moral issue but the quantification is complex because of the imbalance of power and the limited options available to the victim.

Minimum mandatory sentencing guidelines for drug offenders fails the proportionality in self-defence test. The re-offence rate has not been influenced by the longer sentences. There is a disconnect between the prevention of harm and the harm inflicted by the punishment regime.

Often, nations inflict disproportionate harm on segments of their own population or on outsiders. They couch their actions in the language of self-defence, to disguise and justify what is in essence a punitive lesson in subjugation and control and to deter non-harmful actions of which they disapprove. Enshrining non-harmful actions in law to make them illegal does not legitimise infliction of harm to ensure compliance with a bad law.

Principle 5: balance of harms

There are circumstances in which every choice involves inflicting harm. The Balance of Harms principle provides a model for resolving these situations. The Balance of Harms principle requires that where harm is inevitable, then the least harmful option should be selected.

Making that evaluation requires an assessment of the quantum of harms that will be inflicted as a result of each choice. This is no simple matter because of the broad spectrum of harmful actions and the complexity of assessing the quantum of harm in an unbiased way.

Are all lives equally valuable? Women and children are rescued first, a social convention that places women and children above men. Is the life of an octogenarian less valuable than a twenty-year-old? Are people from our tribe more valuable than people who are different?

86　*Harm*

Problem 1: While courts have placed a monetary value on human death and injury, this provides minimal guidance when comparing dissimilar harms – physical, psychological and property.

Problem 2: Similar harms to people should be valued the same, regardless of race or location, but we automatically place a higher value on our own than on others, particularly when the others have been dehumanised.

Problem 3: If one accepts the monetary valuation of people as adequate, then the decision to kill people to save property of higher value is justified.

Problem 4: When damage is distant, or to unborn generations, do you apply a simple discounted cash flow which would diminish the future value of harm from current action to insignificant levels.

Problem 5: How is risk of harm quantified and valued?

Nowhere is the need to assess the Balance of Harms more pressing than in armed conflict. The following situations require an assessment of the harms that will be inflicted by differing actions, including the harm from inaction.

When is it acceptable to kill an enemy combatant?

A.　during armed conflict and there is real and present threat of harm to self and or others;
B.　by sniper fire;
C.　by drone

    i.　when the target is alone;
    ii.　when the target and other fighters will be harmed;
    iii.　when the target and his family will be harmed;
    iv.　when the target and civilian supporters will be harmed;
    v.　when the target and innocent civilians will be harmed.

Do the answers differ when the target is a high-level commander with the capacity to plan and project large-scale harm?

In each of these situations, it is possible to assess the quantum of harm. At its simplest, the question is: How many will be killed versus how many will be saved?

There is a schizophrenia inherent in the idea of 'justifiable killing', or conducting a 'just, righteous, or holy war'. On a mechanistic basis, the Balance of Harms produces a logical, emotion-free answer, because the language of morality or religious belief is removed.

> 'This outrageous explosion of watchlisting – of monitoring people and racking and stacking them on lists, assigning them numbers, assigning them "baseball cards," assigning them death sentences without notice, on a world-wide battlefield – it was, from the very first instance, wrong,' the source tells the Intercept. 'We're allowing this to happen. And by "we," I mean every American citizen who has access to this information now, but continues to do nothing about it.'[3]

An underlying dilemma in the drone debate is the greater weight ascribed to lives of our own compared with the lives of the enemy and their supporters. We ascribe almost no value to the destruction of enemy property.

Proportionality in self-defence is not a sub-set of Balance of Harms. Harming an attacker in self-defence at first glance appears to be a Balance of Harms issue. It is not and cannot be resolved by reference to the Balance of Harms Principle. The decision to harm the attacker in self-defence is simply one of proportionality of response – was the degree of harm inflicted in self-defence reasonably necessary to stop harm being inflicted on you or yours?

5.1 The application of the harm principles

Before examining the sixth Harm Principle, it is useful to explore how the first five principles operate and the limitations of applicability to situations where there is no harm, as defined in section 1 of this chapter, or where the action is directed against something that cannot be harmed.

People, property and the Common are things that can be harmed, but what about more abstract constructs like society, the state and the most perplexing of areas, beliefs and religious faiths.

5.2 Harming society and the state

Can societies and states be harmed by the actions of individuals and groups, whether from within or outside? Clearly, the physical property of the state can be harmed, but what if the conflict with the state is about its legal or philosophical structure?

- When McCarthy prosecuted communists, was he engaging in legitimate self-defence of the capitalist state from the potential harm of the communist ideology?
- When the borders of the state are challenged, does harm result from realigning the border into a more stable ethnic and demographic fit?
- When the philosophy of the ruling party is challenged, as in Tiananmen Square by students wanting a change in the system, is there a threat of harm to the state and if so was the deadly response at Tiananmen Square appropriate?
- When occupying Wall Street, protesters caused disruption and were moved on, what were they harming, or were they protesting against a greater institutionalised harm?

Every armed conflict is harmful and inevitably inflicts death, injury and damage to property. Whether the conflict is internal, as in revolution or civil war, or external cross-border, between nations, directly or through proxies, there is harm. Terrorism, often coalitions of multi-national ideologically inspired

88   *Harm*

irregulars, is a third form of conflict. Regardless of form, they all pose existential threats to the state, society and individuals.

Each side to a conflict attempts to legitimise its claim by relying on mixtures of religious, legal, moral or philosophical constructs. They both claim to be right, good, just and entitled. Those with power and wealth want to keep it, relying on the law which institutionalises their position and claims. The powerless and poor claim unfairness and seek to share more fairly or equitably. When non-violent redress is impossible, they resort to violence. All appeal to some ideal or myth to legitimise their position. All are motivated by our primitive drivers with apparently irreconcilable competing self-interests.

The arguments for or against revolution and change cannot be resolved using the traditional language of right and wrong, legal or illegal, fair or unfair. There is no useful measure for evaluation and resolution when the decision models are cultural, traditional, legal or religious. No side wants to lose, so each resort to wielding power, often resulting in harm.

5.3 Advantages of the harm principles

If an all-powerful alien had the power to resolve these disputes without destruction, it could not do so by utilising the traditional conflict on often contradictory judgement models. By contrast, the Harm Principles would provide a logical structure that can be used in almost every conflict situation. The Harm Principles will not stop the exercise of power in pursuit of self-interest, but they do provide a globally acceptable and understandable language for discussion, negotiation, reconciliation and resolution, when the exercise of power has been put on hold.

The Harm Principles would strike down discriminatory laws that selectively preserved property and favoured one class over another, whether through disenfranchisement or by selective empowering. The Harm Principles would legitimise free speech, which is one of the most powerful tools to limit the abuse of power. The power of money to distort free speech, or shape democratic processes contravenes the Harm Principles. It is easy to connect the dots and for our alien being to deconstruct what we do, consigning actions to categories of not harmful, harmful or not relevant, because the actions are not covered within the Harm Principles.

The Harm Principles empower libertarians to do as they want without restriction, providing they do not harm others, directly or indirectly through systemic distortions. The Harm Principles empower Utilitarians, not so much by maximising the happiness of the masses, but by minimising harm to the individual and the collective. Capitalists can build enterprises, free of constraints, provided that they do not harm.

The Harm Principles delegitimise all forms of despotic self-enriching government except for the mythical unicorn-riding benevolent dictators. Inflicting harm defending the status quo of an inherently harmful regime is not justified within the Harm Principles. Determining the legitimacy of civil disobedience, or civil war, and a government's self-defence response cannot be resolved by reference to religion, philosophy or morality. The laws are useless as they reflect the will of, and are designed to protect, the status quo.

By contrast, because it is neutral and impartial, the Balance of Harms principle provides a mechanism to quantify and evaluate the comparative harms of the status quo and of a proposed new form of state, and the quantum of harms inflicted in transitioning from one form of state to another.

5.4 Exclusions from the harm principles

Clearly, harm can be inflicted on people, property, the Common, the State and even society, but what about ideas, myths and beliefs? Being psychologically damaged is harmful, but what about being offended or upset?

Notwithstanding the universality of harm, not everything we like or everything we may hold dear, can be harmed. Tastes, thoughts, ideas, theories, philosophies, myths and beliefs, including religions, cannot be harmed. The Harm Principles only apply to harms inflicted on people, property and the Common. The state and society fall within the Harm Principles simply because they are collectives of people, not some mythological entity that should be protected in spite of the people.

5.5 Facts, theories and hypotheses

Neither scientifically established theories nor facts can seek protection from the Harm Principles. Scientific proof by its nature is a system that relies on hypothesis, the gathering of facts, experimentation, analysis, challenge, debate, disagreement and the drawing of conclusions, which may later be overturned. There is nothing in the universe that can be spared from debate, analysis, criticism, proof and disproof.

Established 'facts' can be disproved when, with the passage of time, scientific advances provide new insights and knowledge. This method of challenging and demolishing scientific theories and constructs is well catalogued. The black swans discovered by explorers in Western Australia could not be swans because science had declared that all swans were white. There is a long list of fervently held scientific beliefs that have been transformed by advances in science into old wives' tales. What was true became false. Conversely, mythical old wives' tales of the curative power of herbs and potions have proven correct. The cure for malaria is derived from an ancient Chinese method of preparing a herb, yet Western medical professionals vehemently support the allopathic medical model, condemning homeopathic and alternate medical practices as rubbish, until one day myth becomes reality.

The exposed false-facts are not harmed by being debunked, though adherents to them may themselves be discredited, disheartened, offended and emotionally upset through the process of disagreement and disproof. As long as the adherents to the disproven idea, or their property, are not physically or psychologically damaged by attacks on them as individuals in the dispute process, then there is no harm.

90 *Harm*

By contrast, the Christian Church, in declaring certain scientific beliefs as heretical, inflicted great harm, often death, on the 'heretic'. Subsequent validation of the heretical belief as being true could not undo the harm. One problem with contravening religious beliefs stems from the twinning of the primacy of the deity with the unique and central role of man in the universe.

Galileo's heretical view that the Earth was a mere planet revolving in orbit around the sun, and the sun but a speck in the galaxy that was in its turn a mere dusting in the universe, challenged not only core tenets of faith but also the very identity of humans on Earth as divinely special. It was easier to burn the heretic than admit the fallibility of the religious establishment.

Similarly, Darwinian evolutionary theory challenges not just the biblical texts on which the three dominant religions are built, but his theories of the descent of man from the apes destroys totally the unique divine identity and supremacy of man.

The science of the descent of man from the centre of the universe to just another, albeit highly advanced, organism, while deeply upsetting, is not harmful, just inconvenient for the fundamentalists.

5.6 Myths, beliefs and religion

If I believe it will rain today, in spite of or because of the weather forecast, then the simple passage of time will either validate or invalidate my belief. If I believe in fairies, ghosts and other yet-to-be-proven metaphysical constructs, nothing can be said or done that can change my belief. If I profess my belief in alien life, no-one can currently disprove or prove my belief, even though alien beings may exist in other parts of the universe, or in other dimensions that we have not yet discovered.

Religions and other belief systems are different to scientific facts. Beliefs, of which faith is the ultimate sub-set, are not provable or disprovable. One cannot compare, contrast and discern the truth, or otherwise, of one faith from another. Believing in the correctness of one dogma and set of practices immediately invalidates the beliefs and practices of all other dogmas, except where by coincidence they may align. To accept the correctness of the faith of others implicitly invalidates your deeply held faith. Differing faiths, even those with a common heritage, are mutually exclusive and irreconcilable on issues where they disagree.

Religions are the ultimate form of belief. There may be an undisputed historical origin, but the fundamental articles of faith, that of the existence of one or more gods, cannot be proven or disproven.

Disagreeing with the constructs of a religion is similar to disagreeing with a philosophical concept, an idea or theory, or disputing facts or non-religious beliefs. Ideas, philosophies, political persuasions, theories and beliefs are not protected species. They may be debunked, disproven, criticised and even held to ridicule, go out of fashion or completely disappear, but they cannot be harmed within the definition of harm and the framework of the Harm Principles.

The harm principles 91

Disagreeing with religious beliefs is not harmful because beliefs cannot be harmed.

Those with a particular faith believe in their deity despite the multiplicity of faith choices. Articles of faith do not require proof and thus cannot be disproven by argument or disagreement. They are also thus impossible to reconcile.

The problem is not with the differences, but in the emotional and behavioural response to difference. At best, one hopes for passive tolerance of difference. History suggests this is fleeting, and even in the most tolerant of societies the fear of religious difference permeates. Jews, Catholics, Protestants, Muslims and other religions and sects have all been subject to religious intolerance.

Religious difference is compounded by the very nature of religious faith. To some believers, disagreement with their dogma is itself a breach of their religious law. Denying the validity and truthfulness of their holy books or scriptures is construed by them as harming their deity. The greatest type of harm, they believe, is an assault on their deity, hence the capital crime of blasphemy in some states. Slights against the deity have a scale of severity justifying everything from killing to corporal punishment, including mutilation. The elimination of all non-believers is similarly justified because they offend one or other tenet.

Righteous harm is harm inflicted, not in self-defence of a person, property or the Common, but in purported defence of a belief system, or as punishment for those who have transgressed a belief-based rule.

Fervently held religious beliefs are often accompanied by elevated levels of emotion, both in reverence and support of the faith and in condemnation of those who disagree. Those who disagree should be subject to the infliction of righteous harm. Having right on your side, coupled with high emotion, produces the perfect irreconcilable storm.

Inflicting righteous harm to protect a faith does not fall within the ambit of the Harm Principles for two reasons; first, faiths, like beliefs, cannot be harmed, notwithstanding the self-entrenched dogma that says to disagree is harmful; second, the insulted righteous and enraged believer is not harmed, just upset.

Being upset or offended because others disagree with your idea or belief is not a harm. It may not be enjoyable, but the upset is a function of the self-generated fervency of the belief and the intolerance of other ideas. There is a degree of self-inflicted vulnerability in being upset.

There is no harm in preaching the value of one belief over another, even with the object of conversion, providing there is no force or coercion involved, or that the representations of what is required of a convert are clearly explained and understood. However, some faiths and derived legal systems proscribe attempts at conversion. Punishment for a breach is met with righteous harm – violent punishment, often meted out in a summary, extra judicial fashion, led by an incensed mob.

The Harm Principles do not apply to protect voluntary members of a religion, or those who voluntarily choose to visit religious premises, from the rules and controls applied by that religion.

92 *Harm*

The Harm Principles do apply to prevent harm being inflicted by adherents on those who are not part of the voluntary religious association or those wishing to leave. Adherents wishing to enforce their rules and controls on outsiders by inflicting righteous harm are in breach of the Harm Principles.

Unfortunately, fundamentalists of all persuasions are unlikely to abandon their faith and their literal interpretation of long-held covenants and scriptures simply because they become conscious of a harm that will be inflicted in pursuing their belief. That is the very nature of belief and the invulnerability of beliefs to fact and logic.

5.7 The construct, not the person

There is a difference between attacking a religion, its dogma and practices, and harming individuals because of their religious affiliation. Harm to the individual is proscribed by the Harm Principles. People have been and continue to be physically attacked and discriminated against because of their religious affiliation. These actions are harmful.

Attacking the idea is different from attacking the people who hold it, whether as individuals or as a class. There is no harm in arguing, even forcefully, about the validity or otherwise of a religious tenet. By contrast, denigrating the individual and inciting hatred of the person are both harmful. The act of denigration is the first step in the process of dehumanisation. Once dehumanisation is complete, barriers to inflicting harm are broken, setting free our human propensity to harm *others*.

Hatred is an emotional state, often built on a fictional narrative which easily morphs from feeling to action. A close ally of hatred is fear. A mob that hates and fears or a fanatical believer who hates require only low levels of incitement to inflict direct harm. The dehumanising effect of hatred, where the object of the hatred is made into a lesser person or non-person in the eyes of those who hate, allows ordinary people to do terrible things. It is not just for extremists and fanatics. Dehumanisation is carefully scripted into the training of soldiers to enable them to kill the enemy in close-order combat. Without this training, it is much more difficult for soldiers to disassociate the idea of the soldier as a person from that of the depersonalised, demonised enemy.

Incitement is the tool of choice of states to gain popular support for harmful actions. Populist politicians such as Donald Trump appeal to fears and prejudices, promising to keep followers safe from the harm that, without his protection, the 'others' would inflict. To some, Trump's appeal was to enable fearful and marginalised voters on the fringe, to inflict harm by proxy through the power of the elected office.

The linguistic of incitement is not uncommon in corporations. Customers, competitors, and suppliers are depersonalised, making harmful acts easier. In Chapter 2 the concept of the morality mask was introduced. When employees are required to don the prescribed corporate belief system and suspend their personal behaviour guidance systems, they become susceptible to doing harm and feel righteous, simultaneously. The Harm Principles mitigate the evolution of the mask and provide a counterweight to inappropriate values.

5.8 Alignment of the harm principles with religions

There are many requirements set out in different religions that are aligned with the Harm Principles, such as injunctions against killing and stealing. There are also many religious prescriptions that are not in the ambit of the Harm Principles. Actions required to be done in accordance with the faith such as prayer ritual, dress, diet and personal observance may be different from other codes, but there is no harm in the difference or the proscription.

The harm boundary is reached when the ordained precepts and practices harm individuals without the capacity to give real informed consent, such as children and the mentally impaired, or where members who wish to leave the religious group are harmed.

Segregation of men and women during religious service is of itself not harmful, but it presages the approach of an important boundary. If part of the religious code that is voluntarily accepted by congregants is separation, then there is no harm. When the segregation extends beyond the religious practice into the private life, then a different set of issues is raised.

If women are seen as chattels, or lesser, and can be harmed at the whim of the husband or male relative, then there is harm. When sexual discrimination denies a female child an education, another subtler boundary is crossed. Children do not have the capacity to consent to harmful practices. Denying education is harmful to the child. It destroys the potential for higher income from advanced levels of employment. It is a theft of her future property and possibly damaging to her psychologically.

The cloistering of children, male and female, from the outside world, denying them access to knowledge and information with which to make an informed choice when they mature, is a subtle form of harm, as is the effective brainwashing and indoctrination that eliminates any potential to make an informed choice.

Having the freedom to make an informed choice is very different from having notional freedom but inadequate knowledge to make a reasoned decision.

5.9 The righteous infliction of harm

The infliction of harm is not necessarily wrong or evil. Nor is everything evil necessarily harmful. Evil is a social construct. There are many non-harmful behaviours that are deemed evil simply because there is a breach of a religious, social or legal value system. By contrast, cutting off a hand, imprisoning or executing a criminal are all harmful, but sometimes justified by the social system in which the act is carried out.

Ancient religious texts enumerated punishments such as stoning, amputation, mutilation, branding, flogging and beheading. These practices have formed part of the evolution of most societies, but, like the dinosaurs, they passed into

94 Harm

extinction in most countries and cultures. In the West, we no longer routinely torture, and when such practices are exposed they become a major political issue. The rack, thumb screw, burning at the stake and dunking of witches and scolds have passed out of the punishment repertoire. They are not proportionate to the harm inflicted.

The evolution in approach to punishment is a perfect example of how different parts of the world have changed at different speeds and where the conflict of cultures and values collide in a public spectacle. Concepts of punishment and humane treatment of prisoners inform 'modern' jurisprudence, which all align with the Proportionality of Harm principle. Yet, capital punishment is still common.

We castigate and denounce the actions of ISIL in beheading captives as if it was extraordinary barbarism, yet the British beheaded traitors and inconvenient Queens into the seventeenth century. The Japanese Samurai sword was used to behead prisoners through to 1945. The Nazis decapitated over 16,000 ordinary criminals between 1933 and 1945. The French took beheading to an art form with the guillotine, and the death sentence was only abolished in 1981. Beheading in Saudi Arabia is still common. America and China all inflict the ultimate harm in various forms of capital punishment, yet we focus our revulsion on ISIL, who use decapitation perhaps not so much for the harmful nature of the act but because the killing is used as an element of their terror arsenal.

ISIL sees its actions as righteous and the harm they are inflicting as necessary. By dehumanising apostates, they can enslave and kill. There is, in their eyes, no harm. Like the Nazi solider who kissed his child goodbye before returning to his duty at the extermination camp, for them there is no moral question; there was no conflict and there was no perceived harm.

> What difference does it make to the dead, the orphans and the homeless, whether the mad destruction is wrought under the name of totalitarianism or in the holy name of liberty or democracy?
>
> (Mahatma Gandhi)[4]

The attack on *Charlie Hebdo*, a Paris-based satirical magazine that mocked religions in general, and Islam and Judaism in particular, was one of the most poignant (though not the most outrageous) examples of faith-based justification of harm. It may have been in poor taste and even offensive, and in some circles *Hebdo* was claimed (albeit inaccurately) to be 'harmful'. But, even in the extreme, until poor taste and mockery cause psychological damage, they do not fall within the Harm Principles, provided the target is not the person, a characterisation of the person, but the idea.

The Harm Principles do not permit killing because of an affront or an assault on one's beliefs, no matter how fervently held.

Honour killings are a perversion of the principle of inflicting Harm in Self-Defence. Honour killings breach two aspects of the Harm Principles. First, defending against an attack on beliefs is not within the scope of Harm Principles, and second, the response is disproportionate, justified only within the mindset of the believer.

Misuse of the Harm Principles is not limited to religious issues. Nations throughout history have invoked a *duty* to violate the first Harm Principle to defend *vital* national interests. Unfortunately, the definition of what is a defensible national interest has been widely construed to justify invasion to secure raw materials, or to liberate *oppressed* nationals, or even to promote a set of beliefs about a way of life.

The Harm Principles provide a linguistic that is more resilient and less vulnerable to cultural and temporal distortion, and thus more valuable to those who operate across boundaries in our rapidly evolving, globalised world.

Unfortunately, it is the very neutrality of the language of harm that will limit its use by leaders seeking to inflame partisan support to justify harmful actions.

Principle 6: the duty to prevent and reduce harm

> One, a robot may not injure a human being, or through inaction, allow a human being to come to harm.
>
> (Isaac Asimov)[5]

Principle 6 imposes a positive obligation to do good. It is different in class and quality to preventing someone doing harm, which is covered within the five core Harm Principles. The five core principles are founded on the prevention of one person interfering with another. Principle 6 is different, requiring an uninvolved bystander to do good simply because it is possible.

Principle 6 requires a person to go out of their way to alleviate harm, which is a much more intrusive obligation, imposed for no reason other than capacity and proximity. It is easy to argue why preventing harm should be embodied in behavioural principles. It is more tenuous to require a positive action 'for no logical reason'.

There is a substantial leap from the injunction to do no harm to an obligation to prevent or reduce harm being inflicted on strangers. Laws have been enacted in France and Germany requiring third parties to render assistance to those in peril, provided that the person rendering assistance is not placed at risk. Legal action is pending in Germany. An old man collapsed at an ATM. Customers ignored him and used the ATM, which recorded their details. One stranger called emergency services, but the man died. Prosecutors are considering charging those who did nothing.

In other jurisdictions, laws, commonly called Good Samaritan laws, protect those aiding others from legal exposure should something go wrong while assistance is being rendered. This is particularly important for doctors who assist, exposing themselves to lawsuits if things go wrong, even through no fault of their own.

Almost all religions contain obligations for adherents to undertake charitable acts such as a tithe on earnings; or to feed clothe and shelter the poor and those

96 *Harm*

in need; or to offer food and shelter to travellers. But faith-based prescriptions do not provide a globally relevant foundation. For Principle 6 to be valid, there needs to be a foundation independent of religion, culture or law.

The rationale for extending the prohibition against inflicting harm to a positive universal obligation to alleviate harm is not obvious. Most of the language of reducing harm is enmeshed with concepts of goodness and rightness, civic duty or, in the case of corporations, social responsibility.

But why? What drives charitable, benevolent behaviour that is not tied to faith-based prescription?

Both religious orders and charitable secular organisations are supported by individuals donating time and money. Governments aid their citizens and offer aid to peoples of other nations. Even corporations, whose prime purpose is profit, sponsor and support charitable works.

Individuals volunteer and perform charity for many reasons, including: to feel needed, to demonstrate commitment to a cause, to gain skills, as a sense of duty (family, civic or religious), to satisfy family, peer or social pressure, to gain satisfaction and feel proud, to be recognised, to repay a debt or obligation, to help friends, family or community, and even for fun and a sense of belonging.

There is a common thread based in theories of hereditary behaviour. Altruism is popularly understood as being selfless and involving self-sacrifice. The altruistic person expects nothing in return for the charitable action. Neuroscience, to the distress of philosophers who have used altruism as an indicator of the special nature of mankind, or priests who have made charity a key to gaining God's favour, suggests otherwise. The altruist is repaid, not in money, goods or services, but in a chemical hit that makes him feel good, in the same way sex feeling good supports procreation. It is not about selfishness, but about survival.

Darwin and hereditary biologists believe that altruism, along with many other human traits, is inherited as a means of aiding survival and the passing on of DNA. Survival of an individual and their offspring was maximised by belonging to a group or tribe. Membership of that tribe required adherence to a suite of rules and behaviours, one of which was reciprocal altruism. Hunters shared their prey. Farmers shared their produce. Water was collected and shared. Villages provided not just shelter but also collective mutual protection. Every member had a role. Mutuality of interests drove acts of assistance and sharing, which would be repaid in kind, though not necessarily in the same form. Reciprocal equivalence is the basis of markets, which sponsor growth and development.

In villages, reciprocity was visible. Apparent altruism became part of a collective of reciprocal acts. A helps B but may be helped in turn by F. Collective altruism increased the chances of individual, familial and tribal genetic survival. Family collectivism maximised passing on of DNA. Helping your child survive maximised your DNA survival. Helping a brother survive ensured that at least 25 per cent of an individual's DNA would be passed on. More distant relatives contained less and were thus supported less.

Reciprocal altruism has been observed in non-human species where small stable populations made longitudinal observation of inter-relationships possible.

The harm principles 97

Seemingly selfless acts by one member of a colony towards others on closer study were revealed to be predicated on acts of reciprocity by the recipient. If the recipient did not reciprocate, then the 'charity' ceased. A study of bat colonies,[6] where young were raised and fed communally, revealed that when a mother failed to feed the collective nursery, her offspring were selectively excluded from being fed by other adults in the colony. When she resumed collective feeding, the other adults resumed feeding her offspring.

Identifying these connections in modern society is almost impossible. The altruistic driver has been codified in religious obligations for charity, which raises an interesting question: how did the ethic of charity evolve? Where did religious leaders obtain their insight? How did they come to understand that survival through social cohesion was improved when the poor, weak and infirm were supported?

The codification of altruism into religious practice has been beneficial, but codification has had unintended consequences. Altruism is no longer linked to social cohesion but has become more selfish. Charity[7] earns the Gods' favour with the promise of a longer life, or a better afterlife. The reciprocal and temporal links and drivers have been broken. Complex, invisible and then unknown biological drivers were replaced by the simple injunction, 'God said ...'. For the faithful, the motivation of being given a key to the unknown afterlife is a powerful irrefutable motivator. It is the ultimate idea, woven into the most enduring stories and, consequently, having the most persistent power.

There is no one-way altruism in the animal kingdom.[8] It is always reciprocal and always visible. We, however, have lost the visibility. Our societies are too large and too complex. The connection between the donor and the recipient is broken. Charity is often done by proxy, through religious and secular organisations, government and NGOs. The recipients are often too distant to be known and are in no position to offer any reciprocal action.

Proxy charity has not diminished the personal chemical/emotional rewards that flow from individual acts of altruism. The greater the connection and immediacy, the more identifiable the recipient, the greater the individual reward. This may go some way to explain the manipulation by charity marketers when they solicit donations. They make it personal. They link donor individuals to a specific child, not just children; an identifiable animal such as Cecil, rather than just lions in general. You get your personal kit with regular updates on the difference you make to a named animal, village or child.

The more telegenic and photogenic the person or community in need of help, the bigger the impact. The death of thousands of migrants in the Mediterranean had less impact than the tragic picture of one small dead child, face down in the shallows.

Altruism, even with limited reciprocity, has retained its hardwired emotional payoff.

Beyond the tragedy of specific newsworthy natural disasters, the everyday needs of housing, feeding and educating the poor, creating employment and

98   *Harm*

eliminating diseases are all worthy recipients of altruistic acts. But these acts are ubiquitous, impersonal and anonymous, requiring undifferentiated giving. Their very nature limits the immediate payoff for the individual donor. The systemic harm-reduction work that needs to be performed just isn't sexy, which is why the institutionalised work of the Gates Foundation is so important. They tackle systemic issues that are not easily grasped in our imagination. Their work is harder to relate to.

Systemic foreign aid, not tied to specific disasters, is often categorised as misdirected, especially when there are problems at 'home' needing funding. Foreign aid is not one-way and it is not 'pure altruism'. Understanding the reciprocal benefit to donor countries is just more complex and subtle. The payback occurs over generations as the aid manifests itself in changing economic and political structures and the social fabric of recipient countries.

Effective assistance that promotes economic stability will reduce pressure for economic migration. Economic migration, as distinct from refugees fleeing conflict, is an ancient phenomenon, but is now reaching unprecedented levels. We witness the human, social and capital cost on the daily news bulletins as economic migrants, not unreasonably, seek a better life for themselves and their children.

Technology allows everyone to see beyond the village, nation and continent. Every smart phone transmits images of comparative utopias. Social media weave stories of how the journeys can be made and the relative peace, safety and hope for a better life enjoyed by those who took the risks. It is a great idea and a compelling story. Every economic migrant and refugee is driven by the same biological imperatives, to survive. For them the great idea woven into stories and myths is hope. The reality may be different, but as we have seen, facts will not change beliefs and hope is a powerful belief.

From this, one can draw threads, albeit slender, to develop a rationale for Principle 6. Preventing and reducing harm to strangers is founded on the biology of reciprocal altruism, of which there are two parts:

1. Doing good (reducing harm) has chemically induced emotional rewards, beyond any religious promise; and
2. Not fixing systemic harms to strangers will ultimately, in our globalised world, harm us, though not immediately, and perhaps not even in our generation.

There will be opposition to a universal duty to do good. The libertarians will object to an imposition of an obligation, even if fulfilling it makes them feel good. They argue that the decision to embark on an altruistic act should be voluntary. Religions will object because reframing charity as reciprocal altruism debases the spiritual nature of charity, the word of God, the key to the afterlife and the unique nature of mankind.

Economists, who will apply discounted cash flows to obtain the net present value for a harm reduction programme, will be confounded by the uncertainty of outcome and the multi-generational nature of the payback period. Timing and valuation will also deter politicians, who care about the immediate optics and the next election, which will take place long before the benefits from charity materialise.

Surprisingly, for corporations, reducing harm can have tangible rewards in improved staff engagement, reduced turnover, a higher public perception and more social capital, brand value and trust. For corporations, the cost benefit is more tangible because the link between action and *feel good* is clear, particularly if projects are chosen that reinstate the link between the donor and recipient. The staff feel good. They can see the benefit. The recipients feel good and the community they belong to will respond more favourably to the corporation. A virtuous circle that will lead, eventually, to a healthier bottom line.

The operation of Principle 6 is, however, problematic. How much altruistic work is sufficient? *From each according to their ability, to each according to their need*, was a disastrous social philosophy in practice. Socialism failed to recognise the primal driver of survival and its manifestation in self-interest and greed, which in turn fuelled the engines for growth and development.

Prescriptions of a specific percentage, as in some religions, begs the question of why one amount and not another. Once funds are raised, how should they be allocated? To those most at risk of harm; or where the activity will maximise potential harm reduction to ourselves, or simply to maximise how good we feel? Do we support the telegenic? the one's most like us? The innocent child? The victim of acts that frighten and horrify us? Do we invest in economic growth by building infrastructure from schools, hospitals, roads and ports?

There are more questions than answers.

Ultimately, perhaps removing harms, preventing harms and doing good cannot be mandated. Principle 6 thus is included, not as a core principle, but because it completes the circle and hopefully will stimulate debate, inform policy and inspire action for rational, logical and sustainable reasons.

5.10 Harm and the law

> You do not examine legislation in the light of the benefits it will convey if properly administered, but in the light of the wrongs it would do and the harms it would cause if improperly administered.
>
> (Lyndon Johnson)

There is considerable alignment between the drivers for the creation of laws and the Harm Principles. Harm is used in jurisprudence to guide whether an action should be made illegal. For example, the harm caused by the 2008 financial crisis led to a raft of laws to proscribe behaviours that were assessed as causing the harms.

Even a cursory glance at 'good' laws demonstrates that they have at their heart the minimisation of harm by regulating the exercise of abuse of power, whether

100 *Harm*

by an individual, a corporation or government. The weaker are protected from the stronger. Some simple examples illustrate the point. There are laws that:

- Prohibit physical violence, theft or destruction of property;
- Restrict unfair competition and monopoly practices to protect weaker enterprises from unfair practices by powerful competitors;
- Prohibit money-laundering to inhibit the activities of criminal behaviour by making it more difficult for them to access the proceeds of their crime, or tax evasion; and
- Protect the environmental Common;
- Limit politicians abusing the power of their office (constitutions).

The thread is unmistakable. The abuse of power is limited by laws to mitigate harm to the less powerful by those with power.

Once a law is proclaimed, a different set of principles applies. There are rules of interpretation, construction and precedent. Too often, the guiding principle behind the law, i.e. the type of harm it is intended to redress, is lost. Lawyers, and the legal system, examine the narrow interpretation of the law to see whether the law can be construed as applying to a specific action or event. The narrowed focus is applied even in the face of documented legislative intent. The goal is often to find the gap, not apply the intent.

If the prevention of harm was specifically included in laws, it would make it easier to prosecute not just for known, enumerated harms set out in the laws but also for yet-to-be-exploited actions of the type intended by the legislation that result in harm. It would also make it harder to find and exploit any gaps.

5.11 Legal defences in mitigation of harming

The mitigating factors in defence of inflicting harm are well embedded in legal systems:

- Self-defence;
- Intention;
- Accident;
- Negligence;
- Reckless indifference;
- Egg-shell skull;
- Foreseeable consequences.

There is no conflict in applying these defences in both legal and harm theory.

There is no conflict between the Harm Principle and the legal principle of state of mind. The inflicting of harm can be deliberate and intentional, negligent and with reckless indifference, or accidental and inadvertent. Each of these states of mind does not alter the nature of the harm, but only culpability.

The Harm Principle does not limit the ability to create strict liability offences.

5.12 Threat of harm as a tool for social order

Societies use the threat of harm through legally sanctioned punishment of its members to protect other members from being harmed. Societies use the relative vulnerability of members to ensure the security and stability of the society. Societies, through the justice system, inflict pain, restrict liberty, cause suffering and deprive members of their property as punishments for breaching laws.

> We sleep safe in our beds because rough men stand ready in the night to visit violence on those who would do us harm.

Society has the right to inflict harm on those who break legitimate laws to punish criminal behaviour and to act as a deterrent. The quantum of harm inflicted in punishment, however, must be proportional to the harm inflicted. Society does not have the right to inflict harm as a means of seeking revenge or of suppressing actions that are not harmful, such as protest and expressions of disagreement.

Even the most violent of societies, such as street gangs, have codes which minimise the harm administered within their group. Social order is maintained, not because of the benevolent nature of the group, but because of the threat of harm being inflicted for a breach of their code.

Not all order is maintained by fear of harm. Self-interest also informs the conduct of members of societies to preserve the social order. Societies employ positive and negative emotional tools to drive alliance and allegiance – shame, pride, guilt, remorse.

These tap not just into our rational cognitive systems but also into the mechanisms of hereditary biology. Survival of our individual DNA is enhanced by belonging to a clan, aligning and supporting kin, and empowering and following a strong leader who keeps us safe or promises a better, safer future. There is a complex interplay between trust, hope and fear. This amalgam of forces and interactions provides an antidote to the natural beast within.

5.13 The divergence between law and harm

While there is considerable alignment in the drivers for laws to mitigate harm, there are, unfortunately, some laws that are harmful and offend the Harm Principles. These include laws that:

- Discriminate against individuals, or groups;
- Promote the protection of the interests of one class at the expense of another;
- Empower the state to appropriate property without proper recompense;
- Empower officers of the state to act in their own interest, or capriciously in the exercise of their duties; and
- Permit the destruction of the Common.

102   *Harm*

Being lawful does not make a course of action harmless and right, nor does making it illegal imply there is a harm and thus a wrong.

There are also many laws that apply to the form and process to be followed, rather than the substance and consequence of prohibited or required actions. These laws may promote the efficient and effective operation of complex societies: for example, the rules of the road. They may also initiate complex, time-wasting and costly procedures that generate a sub-class of harms that could be called 'process harms', which may result in real harms. For example, when medical advances are unreasonably delayed by unproductive red tape that has little to do with safety and efficacy of treatment, lives may be harmed.

Some laws have unintended harmful consequences. For example, the treaties that recognise national boundaries, on their face, promote global peace and stability and inhibit one nation from intruding across sovereign borders. However, the sanctity of the man-made construct, the myth of the nation state, has had the unfortunate consequence in the Middle East and Africa of dividing or combining ethnic groups into separate newly minted countries to satisfy British or French geo-political aspirations.

Those laws set the scene for many current conflicts as ethnic groups seek national autonomy, often to avoid the oppression that comes from being a minority in their arbitrarily allocated country. Tribalism, linked to ethnicity and religion, is more powerful than lines on a map.

The idea of a tribal or ethnic homeland goes to our most primitive core, yet separatists, often designated terrorists to delegitimise their identity and claims, are repressed violently to maintain an artificial national identity.

National sovereignty, while a useful political construct for leaders, generates a range of harm-threatening sentiment and actions. Nationalism plays to the worst in tribal motivators. Respecting sovereign borders allows harmful regimes to operate with relative impunity from the harm they inflict on their populace, even as they threaten neighbours and the world. It is an inconvenient construct, relied on to justify doing nothing.

5.14 The regulators' dilemma

Regulators are empowered to enforce laws and regulations. The laws under which they operate set out which behaviours are unacceptable, or are required. The dilemma for regulators is their inability to act when their legal mandate does not extend to allow them to stop harmful behaviour.[9]

Regulators have two choices: act beyond their legislated powers to protect the public from harm, or allow the harm to continue. If they adopt the first strategy, at the most basic level they act *ultra vires* – without mandate and authority. Any sanction imposed will be challenged and overturned. More fundamentally, when they act without authority, regulators become institutionalised vigilantes and in doing so threaten the fabric of society. Institutional integrity is the bedrock of our civil societies. The motives may be pure, but that is not sufficient.

If regulators adopt the second strategy of seeking authority through legislative change, harm will be inflicted and the most the regulator can do is issue warnings to the public while they inform the legislature, seeking an extension to their regulatory powers. Both courses of action are undesirable, but the Balance of Harms principle would suggest that the second course of action is less harmful, providing the legislators act in a timely manner.

5.15 The changing social attitude to inflicting harm

Most, perhaps all, societies have at some period in their history institutionalised the infliction of harm. Even forms of legally sanctioned punishment, which would now be deemed cruel and unusual, were promoted in the belief that social order would be threatened without institutionalising the threat of gross harm to limit the random infliction of harm by the general populous.

Exercising power through harming is an ancient tool, with roots in our primitive social and survival drivers. Controlling when harm could be inflicted was incorporated and deeply embedded in religious, philosophical and legal systems, even while the infliction of harm was widely justified by those religions, philosophies and laws. The object of the harm would have been those who transgressed 'laws' and the 'others' of a different race, religion, class or nation, who, having been dehumanised, were not considered capable of being harmed. For *the others*, harm was inflicted without consideration for economic advantage and often for sport and sheer enjoyment.

Societies evolved their attitude to inflicting harm and cruelty. What triggered the change is unclear. For example, in Britain:

- What were the forces that changed public attitudes to spectacles of violence – public hanging, flogging, bear baiting, dog fights – to the more civilised 'blood sports', with rules for controlled violence and the more equal potential for pain and victory such as boxing and rugby?
- What promoted the shift in thinking away from the discriminatory valuation of individual differences based on race, religion or sex?
- What forces made slavery illegal, reduced the glory of colonisation and subjugation of lands and peoples, yet retained the ideal and glorification of the noble, just war?

Some of the influencing factors could have included:

- The popular dissemination of new ideas in philosophy and morality;
- An upwelling of a desire for personal safety accompanied by, or flowing from, new thoughts of the personal right to be safe; and
- The growth of the middle class, who sought to protect their increasing wealth, status and power.

If the selfish protection of property and status is the driving force, then those who have nothing have no reason to support the system that protects the property

104   *Harm*

of those who have, except if the poor believe that one day they or their offspring will have property and status. The recognition that we had common vulnerabilities provided a philosophical basis for systems of control that mitigated harm through the rule of law. Eradicating *unnecessary* systemic and arbitrary harm reduced insecurity and fear of suffering, a perfectly logical self-interested motivation. Thus, the promulgation and enforcement of laws that mitigate harm have been civilising forces.[10]

During the period of great reform, survival, self-interest and selfishness were not lauded as virtues worthy of support from moral philosophers or religions. They relied on 'higher' rationale. While the selfish driver was downplayed, societies evolved as if these forces were operating *sub rosa*. The outcome was that:

> different peoples are organized (so) that they can go about satisfying basic needs and promoting vital interests without harming each other over and over again.
>
> (Andrew Linklater)[11]

The concept of mutual selfishness reached its zenith in the atomic era. Recognition of the capacity for total annihilation spawned a détente, not driven by a meeting of philosophical minds and common ideals, or the rights and virtues of the other side, but the recognition of the existential self-harm that would be inflicted if nuclear arms were used. There was no virtue in MAD (mutually assured destruction), simply a recognition of mutual selfishness as a satisfactory basis for organising international affairs in our missile-connected globalised world. Perhaps the atomic age, with mutual restraint, confirmed that mutually assured destruction is sufficiently powerful to limit the actions of the rational who hate their enemy, but not at the expense of their own existence.

Unfortunately, this simple model is rarely, if ever, applied in its pure form because there is normally an imbalance of power. Those in power have historically developed controls to stop harm to themselves and their sources of power and wealth. Societies and institutions that prospered from a particular ideological, social or legal structure similarly pursued selective controls that contravened the Harm Principles in a totally selfish manner to reinforce protection of harm to their interests.

By contrast, the broader diffusion of power in democratic societies promotes the development of a more (though not absolute or uniform) universally beneficial suite of controls against harm. In this regard, enlightened self-interest is at work. Ensuring that the Harm Principles protect all groups recognises that selectively discriminating against a specific group may be temporally limited. Things change! If it is their group today, then why not my group tomorrow?

Freedom from Harm has been one of the great liberators of economic activity. It is much easier to invest time and money if one believes that there will be no arbitrary acquisition of your property by the government, or destruction of your enterprise by corporations and individuals with greater economic and political power.

Freedom from fear of harm builds trust and trust enables the taking of risk and the pursuit of activities. The safer we feel, the less we need to keep our wealth under the mattress.

Perhaps the ultimate product of globalisation will be the development of a mindset of mutuality and the need to avoid mutually assured harm, if not destruction. Enlightened self-interest, exemplified in reciprocal altruism, may become the driving force, and the Harm Principles the standards by which we engage. Against this, we appear to be entering an age of neo-tribalism, where the forces of international cooperation and globalisation have, at least for the moment, reached a peak. Tribalism, in the form of resurgent nationalism and the pursuit of national self-interest, appears to be on the rise. Simultaneously, we are in a post-rational era where fact and logic are being neutered in favour of rhetoric targeting our primitive drivers of fear of others, tribal trust and the need to band together to survive.

Notes

1 The Greeks owned slaves who could be harmed at the whim of the owner.
2 Person includes groups, corporations and other legal entities.
3 https://theintercept.com/drone-papers/the-assassination-complex/
4 M K. Gandhi, *Peace, Non-Violence And Conflict Resolution: My Non-violence*, compiled and edited by Sailesh Kumar Bandopadhyaya. Ahemadabad: Navajivan, 1960.
5 I. Asimov 'Runaround,' in *I, Robot*. New York: Doubleday, 1950, p. 40.
6 L K. Denault and D A. McFarlane Joint Science Department, The Claremont Colleges
7 Charity is just one of many behavioural requirements.
8 Why Are Animals Altruistic? April 5, 2006 Centre National De La Recherche Scientifique.
9 Malcolm Sparrow's texts – *The Character of Harms*. Cambridge, MA: Harvard University Press, 2008, and *The Regulatory Craft*. Brookings Institution, 2000.
10 Andrew Linklater, *The Problem of Harm in World Politics: Theoretical Investigations*. Cambridge: Cambridge University Press.
11 Ibid.

Part III

Harm and the corporation

6 Drivers of corporate behaviour

Key points:

- Corporate behaviour is shaped not only by the underlying human condition described in Part I, but also by the very nature and purpose of incorporation.

Incorporation and markets negatively impact behaviour by:

- Separating shareholders from control and responsibility;
- Insulating executives and staff from the consequences of risky behaviour;
- Setting unreasonable growth and profit targets to grow shareholder wealth.

The size and structure of large corporations negatively impact behaviour by:

- Placing layers of leaders between staff and the ultimate leaders;
- Creating distorting layers of clay;
- Building destructive tribal silos;
- Expecting difference in cultures to be overcome by policy and code.

The human condition operates inside the corporation to negatively impact behaviour by:

- Distorting loyalty to leaders, tribes and goals;
- Tying bonus structures to metrics that give little weight to behaviour – the what overwhelms the how;

110 *Harm and the corporation*

- Survival – keeping the job;
- Fear; and
- Needing to belong.

The corporate systems and processes for rule setting, communication and training erroneously assume that fact and logic will change behaviour.

The cataclysmic destruction of trust in corporations is a direct result of corporations behaving badly. The public, governments and regulators are angry and frustrated. The public has lost faith in the integrity of corporations and their political counterparts. Few believe corporations act in anything but their own, profit/bonus-driven, self-interest. The financial turmoil and business scandals of the last decade have touched everyone. Yet for all the rhetoric, it appears to many that nothing has changed.

Businesses operate under formal and informal licences from the community. There is a compact. In return for granting the licence to operate, communities expect to receive quality goods and service and reasonable and fair treatment. They expect the corporation to behave respectfully as a member of the community. When the social compact is ignored, trust in the corporation is lost.

Unfortunately, the loss of trust does not show up directly in the accounts. There is no line item in the balance sheet. Wave after wave of scandals generate headlines, contrition, promises, a tsunami of regulation and billions in legal fees and fines. The increase in regulation and regulatory intervention, in turn, generates a flurry of governance, risk, compliance and ethics (GRCE) activity, but with limited effect on real corporate attitudes, behaviours and the quantum of harm inflicted on the community.

Boards and CEOs understand the central importance of trust to profitability. They invest heavily in traditional control tools such as codes of conduct, values, policies and procedures, which are then communicated, inculcated by training and finally monitored by Compliance and Ethics departments, who in turn may be monitored by board committees. Critically, the rebuilding of trust does not match the effort and cost.

With so much effort, why is there so little impact?

The cynic would answer that the changes are cosmetic – form over substance; defensive – done to protect leaders from regulatory accusation; and token – leaders give mixed signals – comply, wink, wink. Compliance is subordinated to meeting targets. There is some truth in this, but it is not the whole story.

Corporations, like individuals, are impacted by myriad forces that influence behaviour: laws, geography, politics, economies, demographics, leadership, community, values, beliefs, cultures, etc. Commercial enterprises have the additional complexity of operating in markets subject to powerful ever-shifting forces of supply and demand, competition, technological change and the need to generate growth and profit, all in a shifting tide of politics, law and regulation.

The very nature of corporations impacts how they behave. Corporations are:

a. Legal fictions, that owe their existence to a legal framework;
b. Owned by shareholders; and
c. Directed by boards and executives who may not necessarily be shareholders.

But a corporation, while having legal status and an identifiable guiding mind, is not a monolithic structure, where commands from the top are implemented exactly as intended in all corners of the operation. This is more the exception rather than the rule because of the fourth factor. Corporations:

d. Do things through the actions of employees, from the most senior executives to the persons cleaning customer-facing areas or disposing of waste.

It is the collective actions of employees, acting in concert or alone, that determines what is perceived as corporate behaviour. Changing corporate behaviour requires an understanding of all the behavioural drivers of individuals set out in the previous chapters, applied in the context of the artificial corporate environment.

By the end of this chapter you will understand:

* The impact of incorporation on mindset and behaviour;
* The problems of structure, size and distance;
* The intersection of personal and corporate values;
* The expression of human primal drivers in the corporate setting.

6.1 The impact of the legal fiction

A corporation is a legal fiction, given substance by the regulatory framework of the society in which it operates. Incorporation provides an excellent foundation for the agglomeration of capital, the hiring of staff and the execution of activities.

Once upon a time, long, long ago, when the world was simpler and communication was by spoken or written word, entrepreneurs raised capital by issuing shares in their venture. Investors, sometimes more aptly called speculators because of the high-promise, high-risk ventures, understood where their investment was intended to be applied. Then as now, funds were diverted by fraud and resources were wasted by mismanagement, but in some cases the venture literally and metaphorically struck gold and paid off.

112 *Harm and the corporation*

The lucky investors recouped their funds by receiving income in proportion to their share – their dividend – and from on-selling their shares to others wanting to participate in the future income and growth of the venture.

Investing in incorporated entities is not a modern phenomenon. During the Roman Republic, the state contracted out many of its services to private companies. These companies were similar to modern corporations in that they issued shares to the public and the price of stocks fluctuated, presumably reflecting the fortunes of the company. Jump forward to France in 1250. Shares in a local milling cooperative, the Société des Moulins du Bazacle, were traded at a value that depended on the profitability of the mills owned by the society.

English joint-stock companies emerged in the seventeenth century. The English (later British) East India Company was granted a Royal Charter by Elizabeth I to promote trade in India. It was owned by multiple investors. This model was quickly emulated, and the principle extended by the Dutch in 1602 with the formation of the Dutch East India Company. The great Dutch innovation was the ability to trade the shares on the Amsterdam stock market, which enhanced the ability of joint-stock companies to attract capital from investors, who could now easily dispose of their shares. The Dutch East India Company became the first multinational megacorporation. Between 1602 and 1796 it traded 2.5 million tons of cargo with Asia on 4,785 ships and sent a million Europeans to work in Asia.

The innovation of joint ownership accelerated Europe's economic growth because the technique of pooling capital provided the finance to build ships, purchase stock and share risk through pooled insurance, the model used by Lloyds of London. What was common in all these ventures was the relatively close link between ownership and management, the capital employed, the activity of the company and the value of the enterprise through the share price. The share value reflected the real and expected earnings of the company, adjusted for risk.

The valuation by the market was not always logical and rational. It appears that humans are willing to gamble, to take risks, to increase their fortune, and their willingness to gamble is influenced by crowd behaviour. The more the buzz, the more the excitement, the more they want to join in and belong and the more they are willing to pay to play. Speculation drove irrational price gains, with the unfortunate occasional bursting of speculative bubbles, also first introduced to the world by the Dutch through the Tulip bubble of 1637.

Jump forward a few centuries. We still gamble, but the vital connections between capital, ownership, control and the enterprise have been eroded, to the point of vanishing. Corporations have, like sentient robots, taken on a life of their own. The legal fiction has evolved far beyond the intention of raising capital and trading shares to invest or recoup investment.

What we have now are markets that operate independently, driven by sentiment and manipulative trading. The market myth so central to modern economies has lost much of its validity, but we cannot let the public know the Emperor is naked. Today, shares are traded independently of underlying fundamentals.

Drivers of corporate behaviour 113

Traders don't care which way the market moves as long as it moves and they are on the right side of the bet. Short selling can kill a company while traders make a killing. The market has great influence on how boards and executives think and behave. The ramifications are enormous, as the largest corporations are wealthier and more powerful than many countries.

6.2 Ownership and control

We all understand that corporations have owners. The owners appoint boards and, in theory, through their boards,[1] have the power to shape and direct the organisation as they see fit. The boards in turn hire and fire the most senior executives, who are contractually bound to execute the decisions of the board. The senior executives similarly hire and fire staff in a cascade, reaching to the lowest levels and furthest corners of the organisation.

In small organisations, owners, directors and executives may be the same people, simplifying the chain of command and reducing the loss of 'signal integrity' from owner to action. The forces on executives differ. Privately owned companies, large and small, are not subject to share-market short-term drivers. Goals may be more than just quarterly growth and profit. The timing, direction and processes reflect the personal motivation of the owner/directors.

By contrast, the market ownership model of corporations has generated a philosophy that the primary purpose of corporations is to maximise the wealth of shareholders, through dividends and/or increases in share price. This is a critical root cause influencer of executive behaviour.

Management theorists and the market accepted that the best way to grow shareholder value was to incentivise executives. Two forms of incentive became popular: making executives (and to a lesser degree staff) shareholders – a longer term incentive; and second, tying executive and employee income to corporate performance through the payment of annual bonuses. The theory behind this was simple. *If we do well you do well.* Unfortunately, there is a mismatch between timescales. Major investment decisions take years to mature, but markets operate quarterly, with a nod to the future – reluctantly, full year numbers, rarely with a three-year or more horizon. The result has been incentives tied to short-term, current-year profitability to match the market cycle, not the investment's needs.

Bonuses have failed as a driver of good behaviour. The outcome was predictable. The rational result of a misguided incentive has been the development of a culture of self-serving decisions and behaviours to maximise bonuses, salaries and promotion. Profit maximisation, especially short-term, has shifted the balance of decision making from long-term strategic to short-term tactical to satisfy ever-shortening demands from analysts, who make and inform the market.

The combination of shareholder demand for profit and executive pursuit of bonuses has proven to be a sometimes-toxic combination that shapes and continues to shape executive decision making and behaviour, and by consequence the actions of staff and the corporation as a collective. Highly motivated

114 *Harm and the corporation*

executives, focused on personal gain and power, have taken increasingly risky decisions, cut corners and even, from time to time, willingly breached the law.

How often have you heard over the last decade, executives bleating to the media: 'We did nothing wrong? It was legal.' There are legion employees who could testify to the pressure to find and exploit legal loopholes and to follow orders, even if the orders seemed wrong – driven by the imperative to meet or exceed targets, forecasts and analyst's expectations.

This goes a long way to answer the ages-old question, '*why do good people do bad things?*' They do so because it is rewarded financially and because it is part of the tribal way we do things.

6.3 The corporate veil

An integral element of the legal fiction of incorporation is the doctrine of the corporate veil.[2] The concept is that the legal identity and legal liabilities of the corporation are separate from those of its shareholders and employees. This separation protects shareholders and employees, including senior management and boards, from personal exposure. This is a logical extension of civil and criminal law, where individuals are generally not liable for the independent actions of others. There is no doctrine in modern civilisations of collective responsibility.

Who would work for a corporation if individual employees were liable for the actions of other employees? Not only is there separation of ownership from employment, but most employees have no personal power to materially impact the collective behaviour of the corporation, or the individual behaviour of fellow employees. The corporate veil is *a necessary evil*. Why evil?

The lack of personal liability has the potential to distort behaviour. In Chapter 1 we explored how fear of bad things happening is a critical element of our primitive survival mechanism. When the risk (fear) of personal liability is removed, so is the inherited driver that would otherwise limit risky behaviour.

Many executives, in pursuit of profit and bonus growth, have taken risks, not with their own money or with personal exposure, but with shareholder capital, employee security, customer loyalty and community trust. This is an unintended behavioural consequence rooted in the very nature of incorporation, reinforced by the bonus culture.

Employees are rarely prosecuted for the criminal behaviour of the corporation.[3] They do not have civil liability for product defects, nor mis-selling. Rarely have they had to pay back bonuses after their inappropriate behaviour is exposed. If the company makes a loss, or is sued, the company must pay reparations. It is not, by and large, the employees' problem.

Employee actions are not risk-free. They risk loss of bonus, lack of promotion and in the worst case being fired. Yet if they do not take the risk, make the profit, hit the target, be a team player and follow orders, they will not receive the bonus or be promoted, and they risk being fired for non-performance. The problem for employees is that their sword of Damocles is two-edged. They can be damned if they do and will be damned if they don't. The conundrum for employees is limited to a shift in timing. Refusing to do the wrong thing gets them fired or side-lined immediately. Doing the wrong thing may have repercussions sometime in the future, or not at all. When faced with this Hobson-like choice is there any wonder that otherwise honest employees do nothing and say nothing. The outcome is harm to customers and shareholders and often the community.

6.4 The problems of scale and structure

We are biologically programmed to respond to signals from our leaders and our tribe. The signals are a mix of verbal content (data and information) and process – how the message is transmitted. We trust and follow strong congruent leaders who make us feel safe, especially in times of perceived threat.

The same is true in corporations. In small corporations, it is easy for the leaders to be visible, to have personal communications, where the whole message, comprising content and processes, is clear.

In large corporations, particularly those with multiple locations, even within one country, two forces are operating against our biological followship mechanism – distance and structure.

Tyranny of distance

Distance makes it difficult, if not impossible, for the whole message to be received. Modern technology has improved but not solved the problem. It is now easy for leaders to transmit the message using multiple media such as personalised emails, town halls, video conferencing, webinars and tweets. Yet even with high frequency and 100 per cent accuracy in transmission of content, the message more often than not gets distorted.

One-size-fits-all messaging is difficult to compose. At what level should the message be pitched? Too high and complex makes it hard for all employees to work out what is intended. Dumbed down and simplified generates ambiguity and lack of clarity. Universal communication packages ignore the differences in background, culture, education, hierarchy and function of modern complex corporations. Employees feel the messenger is distant. They can feel leaderless and so disengage from the corporation, transferring identity, engagement and loyalty to their proximate leader.

Distortions from structure

The second factor is structure. Every organisation, whether incorporated or not, has structures which involve layers and groups. The layers are designed to manage span of control and are grouped vertically for efficiency of function. The result is a series of layer cakes that sit side by side.

Each horizontal layer has its level of management. Between the corporate leader and the proximate manager may be many other managers. This plays

116 *Harm and the corporation*

directly to the biology of whom we choose to follow. Do we follow the distant CEO or the managers who have our life in their hands? Will the CEO keep us safe, or will I be better off following the instructions of my immediate supervisor – my proximate manager?

Tribalism dictates we follow the leader of OUR tribe, which, unless the CEO is exceptional, will be the proximate leader or the next leader up. Mountains have been written on effective span of control. There is less written on maximising depth of influence through multiple layers. How many layers can a CEO be expected to lead effectively? It depends on the individual, but more on how the distribution of power, control and communications is managed.[4]

Vertical layers can be just as destructive as geographic distance to the effective transmission of meaning. Anecdotal evidence suggests that there exists in some corporations a semi-permeable layer, varyingly described as permafrost, layer of clay or the lead barrier. In essence, once a message reaches *the layer*, it does not get through as transmitted. Something happens when top-down messages and instructions, particularly on behavioural drivers such as values and business principles, hit this twilight zone.

As a consequence, the great intentions and instructions from the board, CEO and senior management are diluted, distorted, reframed and even subverted as they flow down the organisation. The inhabitants of the permafrost reinterpret what was intended. They change the message to suit their own objectives and drivers. Nowhere is this more prevalent than when instructions from above appear to have the potential to impact negatively on sales and profit, or require extra work, or work to be done differently.

Local managers, if challenged, find reasons why what was said was not what was meant. Commonly used rationale includes:

- They don't understand the situation here.
- We have always done it this way (not their way).
- Yes, that is what they said, but this is what they meant. Wink. Wink.
- If we are going to make target, this is what we must do.
- There is no time, budget.

Welcome to the managerial twilight zone where different laws of physics apply, distorting the orderly behaviour of employee planets around their leadership Sun. The power of the corporate leadership team, like the Sun, keeps the planets in orbit. But as on Earth, it is the relatively tiny, but proximate, Moon, that influences the tide.

Lower level staff ultimately follow the instructions and emulate the behaviours of their more proximate leaders. What may be clearly said at the top is not understood universally nor implemented homogenously throughout the organisation. Leaders naively believe that because clear instructions have been given, they can assume that the fleet has changed course, and are surprised when the distant parts of the fleet continue to sail into the minefield. The result is increased exposure and reduced risk control, the opposite of what was intended.

This is not the same problem as the giant brontosaurus whose brain signals took minutes to reach the tail. Rather, in large corporations it is as if there are mid-brains in the body of the beast that interrupt, override and act independently of the central control system.

6.5 The quantum multiplier influence of globalisation

To the problems of distance and structure must be added the impact of globalisation.

Regulating human behaviour for the good of the community has been and remains a persistent and problematic issue. There is no one perfect solution. This is evidenced by the endless arrays of religious codes, social mores and documented laws that societies have created to bring order to their worlds. Anarchy is not our preferred native state. Tribalism and the exercise of power within the tribe are. Societies evolved controls to match their changes, growth, increasing complexity and reduced homogeneity.

This timeless dilemma is reaching its apogee. Globalisation and connecting technologies have brought unprecedented complexity. The impacts are consequently greater, rippling like a wave around the globe. The growing convolution of societies, economies and modes of interaction requires a more rapid and flexible system of regulation and control, which is not currently being met through traditional national legislative and regulatory systems. The battle over Britain staying in the European Union is symbolic of the tension between globalising forces and national identity. We are tossed and battered by the currents and waves of globalisation. At heart, we seek tribal islands where we feel safe, regardless of the commercial reality. This powerful collision of forces drove the most unbelievably divisive US presidential election between Hillary Clinton and Donald Trump. It drives the growth in neo-nationalism and isolationism, of both the left and the right.

The interconnectedness of societies across distance brings with it the need for behavioural principles that are independent of local cultures and histories. When colonial enterprises, such as the Dutch East India Company, operated in ways we would now label cruel and even criminal, there was no 24/7 live video feed, no twitter debate, no social media coverage, no massive leaks of information. If anything, the colonial enterprises were lauded, the successful individuals lionised and young men set off to make their fortune in the far-flung outposts of the corporations. In many instances, these corporations were the law, a law unto themselves.

Today, however, the colonial enterprises are no longer the sources of order, control and culture in the outposts in which they operate. Their historic behaviour, once lauded, would today be decried. True, multinationals still have enormous financial and political power and influence, but they can no longer act with impunity. The changing globalisation dynamic is shifting the balance from exercising power to earning trust.

118 *Harm and the corporation*

The CEO of global corporations must add the impact of differences in laws, practices, heritage and cultures in each of the countries in which they operate to the problems introduced by geographic distance and vertical layers. Each of these additional factors plays into the hands of local managers who can add local issues and characteristics to their rationale for selective implementation of central messages and policies. The local manager can quite legitimately raise issues of conflicts of laws, differences in business practices and the impact of their culture on the way things get done.

The dilemmas for leaders of non-criminal global businesses are:

- We want to be trusted, but how do we earn and keep trust with increased visibility and 24/7 news?
- What standards should we apply to our corporate behaviour?
- How do we get all staff to understand what is acceptable behaviour and what is not?
- How can we develop a coherent, pervasive mindset and behaviours that allow us to operate trans-nationally and globally in regions and countries with differing cultures and laws?

In Chapter 2 we concluded that the law does not provide a foundation for determining what is universally right and wrong, because what is legal depends on geography and point in time. For multi-nationals, simply instructing staff to obey the law raises for staff the legitimate questions: 'Which laws? The laws where the parent corporation is incorporated? The local laws? The laws of the contract?' This is a high-risk issue that complicates behavioural drivers.

Multi-nationals are vulnerable to regulators in multiple jurisdictions. It is not as simple as the country of incorporation, or operations, but can extend to the jurisdiction of customers and suppliers with whom they do business, the products and services they trade and the currencies in which they transact.[5]

Often multi-nationals adopt compliance with the strictest legal regime as their corporate standard, particularly when the strictest regime is accompanied by a powerful activist regulator such as the US Department of Justice, which will pounce on breaches of US Federal law, even when carried out in remote corporate outposts.

Adopting a higher compliance standard is intended to keep the corporation safe, but can have the unintended consequence of requiring local operations to adopt a behavioural standard higher than that demanded by their local laws and regulations. The local competitors, who operate only in one country or region, will not be governed by the same regulatory pressure. The competitors can thus operate more freely at lower standards of behaviour, which results in a competitive disadvantage for the local operations of the multi-national.

This is most pronounced in the finance industry. The global bank must be more intrusive, requiring proof of identity and the source and application of funds to prevent crime or profit from the proceeds of crime. In many emerging markets, providing such information is anathema. Global banks very often cannot, therefore, offer the same products, or do business with some black-listed customers, unlike their purely domestic rivals in the emerging market place.

Applying Western laws against bribery and corruption in some emerging markets runs into conflict at two levels; the relatively benign gift giving and entertaining common in some cultures; and the more pernicious environments of endemic corruption. Both are prohibited by Western laws and actively prosecuted by regulators.

Local management and staff feel disadvantaged in these markets. It is harder to make targets, sales and bonuses. It takes longer and can even be impossible to receive permissions, permits and win contracts. Business is harder. These are powerful forces that local managers can co-opt in explaining to staff that what was issued from head office is window dressing for regulators and for divisions that operate in other countries. The managers pay lip service, and explicitly, but more often implicitly, direct their staff to ignore the imposed edict and to carry on as usual.

The board and senior management believe they have done their duty in having created the right policies, procedures and systems, which have also been communicated and taught. They have the e-learning attendance reports to prove it. The reality is too often different.

In the local managerial twilight zone, not only do local managers have the power of presence, but they can call on two of the most powerful behavioural drivers: us and them, where the them is the rest of the corporation; and survival, not in the primitive existential sense, but in the commercial market place, as measured by sales, growth and profitability.

In post-breach reviews, the issue of local difference is often raised in defence of an otherwise proscribed course of action. It is never a justification, but it is a powerful reminder of the forces at play to distort and neuter good intentions from the top.

6.6 The impact of human nature on corporate behaviour

In previous chapters, we discussed:

- The hereditary nature of behaviours and in particular, the role of tribes, leadership and followship in aiding survival;
- The schema that codified how we should behave – ethics, culture, beliefs, faith and the law; and
- The impact of trust and distrust on how we interact.

Every one of these forces is at work within the corporation. Corporations have the characteristics of societies. They have members, who are grouped in one or many tribes. Each tribe has a leader and followers. Each member of the tribe has a primal drive to survive which is aided by belonging to the tribe. The corporate society stipulates its values, dictates behavioural norms, sets rules and codes and

120 *Harm and the corporation*

develops a culture that supports the desired behaviours. Within the corporation at tribal and individual levels there are varying degrees of trust and distrust.

There are, however, fundamental differences between the natural social world and the artificial world of the corporate legal fiction. The legal fiction is not a mirror universe that emulates the natural world's behavioural models, yet employees are required to move seamlessly between the two worlds. Those who manage the artificial corporate world rarely have insight into the transitional differences experienced by their staff. They assume seamless transition and adoption of the corporate way. The structure of corporations distorts the nature of leadership and, unlike the tribal natural world, the survival and prosperity of the corporation may not always align with, or promote, the survival of the individual.

6.7 Leadership and followship – the power of the alpha

Leaders lead.
People willingly follow real leaders, but obey managers.

We are biologically programmed to follow the leader. The effect is compounded when leadership is formalised in organisational hierarchy and leaders have power over personal survival factors such as promotion, continuity of employment and salary. Aligning oneself to a powerful corporate leader, whether at the highest level or an immediate manager, is an inherited response aligned to survival. It is not simply the logical following of orders, but a deeper embedded phenomenon.

Looking to a leader for behavioural signals is an inherited legacy from our primitive ancestry. We see this in studies of animals, particularly of our evolutionary cousins, monkeys and apes. Their behaviour provides insights into how we respond to the proximity of power and control; threat and reward; belonging and isolation; subservience and following orders. We may clothe human behaviour in cerebral logic, but beneath the logic, non-conscious forces operate.

Staff look for messages from their leaders, who consciously and subconsciously send signals through multiple independent channels:

- What I say;
- What I expect;
- What I do;
- How I do;
- How I assess, judge and hold accountable;
- How I look (non-verbal messages).

All of these conspire to form what employees actually believe. When all of these are consistent and align with the values, strong signals flow down the organisation. There is congruence. Staff want to be able to believe that:

- Leaders live the values.
- The values apply to everyone.
- Everyone at every level is held accountable for breaching the values.

Doubt and non-adherence proliferate when the leaders' actions fail to align with the values. Lip service at the top breeds lip service in the ranks. Leadership does not stop at the CEO or the executive team but operates at every level of manager and supervisor.

We are finely attuned to the non-verbal messages in communication. Early studies estimated that less than 10 per cent of meaning was transferred by words.[6] This has substantial implications for large corporations where dissemination of behavioural requirements is primarily through words, albeit delivered through multiple media. We are becoming more digitally dependent for communication, seduced by the low cost and apparent efficiency.

The rate of change in communication technology has far outstripped our biological evolution. We still respond more to the personal, though the role of social media in forming digital tribes and virtual families may change the equilibrium point. We have not yet calibrated the power of virtual smiles, hugs, emoji and emoticons. They are ubiquitous in social media, conveying considerable, if sometimes ambiguous, meaning, but have yet to find their way into formal corporate communications.

The structure of corporations necessitates layers of leadership, where the corporate alpha leader relies on subordinate levels of obedient leaders to implement instructions and reinforce communications. The consequence for the digitally dependent alpha is that the proximate manager becomes the effective alpha for employees within their span of control.

If the proximate alpha aligns with the titular leader, everything works and messages from the top arrive with minimal distortion at the bottom. However, when the local alpha has a different agenda, the top-down messages and instructions run the risk of being distorted or ignored.

This evolutionary behavioural legacy of responding to the effective alpha leader cannot be overcome by glossy word-based, logical rules, codes and missives from afar, or disembodied teleconferences, e-learnings, video messages and all the standard tools plucked from the communication specialist's handbook.

The local alpha has discernible power to impact on career, salary and the less tangible power to influence followers' sense of wellbeing. The local alpha can control interactions to make the environment positive, or breed internal competition and factions. He has power to provide positive or negative feedback. Critically, the proximate manager can, through the power of non-verbal communications, distort messages downward while paying lip-service to them upward.

6.8 The layers of clay

The larger the corporation and the greater the number of managerial layers, the greater the potential for the *clay effect* to take hold. Clay is a wonderful

122   *Harm and the corporation*

material. In different forms, it can be used to line dams to make them waterproof. Other clays are used in filters, to selectively remove particles. In organisations, the clay effect is deleterious. Managers too often selectively block or filter messages intended for their subordinates. Motivation varies but commonly includes:

- Disagreement with the message;
- Belief their staff don't need it, can't understand it, can't handle it.

In its most pernicious form, managers block messages heading upward to:

- Avoid exposure of problems;
- Keep control or ownership of an idea.

The consequences include staff:

- Doing the wrong thing, believing that it is what is required;
- Disengaging because of feelings of frustration, lack of trust, underappreciation, lack of respect.

Responsibility for the failure of the message lies not just with the layers of clay. Senior managers, pressed for time, erroneously believe that the messages so carefully scripted and produced, expensively packaged and universally distributed, were heard and understood by all and everything is fine. Bread has been cast on the water, so why are the fish still hungry?

Just because it is said doesn't mean it is heard, let alone understood. Even if it is heard, without the active engagement of middle managers it will rarely be acted on. In parallel, the layers of clay inhibit upward feedback. For all his failings, Steve Jobs made sure ideas could flow up and down rapidly and unfiltered. It was, and still is, one of Apple's great strengths.

The clay effect is not limited to transmission of values. It negatively impacts understanding of corporate strategy, changes in tactical direction, and messages about risk, compliance and remuneration. It limits the identification of both problems and solutions. This phenomenon has been identified time and time again in workshops I have conducted, with over 100,000 attendees across more than sixty countries and many industries. In nearly every case both problems and potential solutions were known and identified, but the clay effect meant they were never heard.

The Engagement Cascade™[7] has been proven to reduce the impact of the layers of clay. The nature of the Engagement Cascade™ also ensures alignment and commitment top-down and has built-in feedback so leaders can keep track of how people are currently thinking and feeling, without the delay and costly imposition of annual culture surveys. Culture surveys are important, but are too infrequent to provide continuous feedback to managers or to provide employees with a feeling that they are really being listened to.

6.9 Survival instinct inside the corporation

We are biologically programmed to survive to pass on our DNA. This ancient force expresses itself in several ways even in our technically driven, legalistic corporate world. We compete with our peers for promotion, when cooperation is what the corporation needs. We give allegiance and act to support the leader we think will aid our promotion. We act to deliver job security, for the long haul, but also for maximising immediate reward, including feelings of approval from leaders and peers.

Common behavioural manifestations of these drivers include:

- Pursuit of bonuses at the expense of the corporation's long-term interests;
- Acting against the corporation's published values and codes of conduct following orders from the proximate leader, or pursuing personal interest;
- Denigrating colleagues to further personal promotion and ambition.

The survival needs of the corporation do not always align with those of its tribal members. The fractious history of labour relations reflects this. Corporations want growth and maximised profitability. Employees want job security, a safe, conducive environment in which to work and the maximum possible income. There is, therefore, a natural antagonism and source of conflict in the management–staff relationship.

Members of corporate tribes are sacrificed – fired, burnt out and exploited – for the benefit of the corporation. Historically, this was generally not the case in tribes but was not unheard of. The closest real world analogy was the practice of some tribes to leave members to die, or be killed, when the member became too ill, badly injured or infirm with age.[8] This was necessary so that the tribe could survive. It was a recognised and accepted part of tribal life.

The corporate equivalent is less clear. The division of tribal resources – salary, perks, contractual protection – is not uniform. The powerful have disproportionately more benefits and more protection. Even when fired, the elite receive their golden parachute, which provides an easier, less brutal exit. The exploitation of labour, of the less powerful, while mitigated by labour laws and the power of collective bargaining by unions, continues in corporations and is a source of friction.

This divides employees into categories, those with power, who are seen as the embodiment of the corporation, and everyone else. This is simplistic and not true of all corporations, particularly the new breed of internet-based corporations; however, it is a useful starting point. It explains why so much effort is spent creating a corporate identity as a form of tribe to which employees can feel some sense of belonging, thereby masking the lack of alignment of corporate and individual survival objectives.

While corporate writers co-opt Darwin's survival of the fittest theory to justify competitive combat in both the market and within corporate hierarchies, they miss that the underlying purpose of tribes was to protect their members. This was

124 *Harm and the corporation*

why you belonged – to survive, to reduce fear. To do this you had to trust, not just in the leader, but in fellow members, that they too would adhere to tribal values and customs.

When corporate values and customs breed unhealthy competition and distrust, the fabric of the tribe will disintegrate at the emotional level, even while the structure remains in place. Competition to survive decreases cooperation and innovation within teams. Trusting, cooperative teams produce more because they are not worried about whose idea is used, but whether it is the best idea. This was Steve Jobs' genius. He wanted the best idea to survive.

6.10 Tribalism within the corporation

Some of the most influential, although not necessarily the most financially successful, leaders build tribalism and play on tribal loyalties to get things done. They exploit our innate need to belong. They know that employees who identify with the tribe are more loyal, question instructions less, overcome difficulties more easily and cooperate more freely. Tribal mastery is aligned to charisma and cultism. Followers operate on feelings, as well as logic.

Corporate tribes have recognisable behavioural norms and characteristics. There is a tangible look and feel that is, not always but often, accompanied by symbolism and artefacts, which unify the tribe, distinguishing it from other tribes. Members are proud of their tribe, what it does, what it stands for and how it does what it does. Tribalism is a powerful unifying force. It can also be divisive.

To facilitate span of control and efficiency, corporations are divided vertically into silos, often structured around products and functions. The stronger the tribal identity in the silo, the greater the propensity for the silo to behave in its own interest, at the expense of the corporation. The result is an increase in noise in communications. Signals and messages are less clear. Cooperation declines, unless it is silo serving. Agreement and disagreement become more pronounced, aligning along silo boundaries.

Measuring tribalism is thus important. But measuring your *tribal score* is too primitive for the politically correct world of human resources management. Engagement is the management-speak buzz-word for tribalism. Engagement will be revisited later in the coverage of traditional tools and measures.

6.11 The impact of the dual worlds on behaviour

We all operate in multiple worlds with multiple constructs that give us identity. There is only one unifying construct. We are all *homo sapiens*, resident on Earth, with a common genetic ancestry. Beyond that there is infinite divergence. Within the Earth, we have countries, cities and suburbs, each of which impacts our identity and sense of tribe belonging. Alongside and independent of the geographic boundaries are the macro social groupings of religion, race, gender, age and sexual orientation.

There is little value in cataloguing all the myriad layers and intersecting groupings. How we gain our identity – perceive ourselves, changes with age and activity. Single, married, in a relationship. Straight or gay. Academic nerd or sports jock. Wealthy or poor, etc, etc, etc.

What is important is to recognise that employees are not homogenous. They arrive at the front door of the corporation with a continually evolving identity, yet magically as they cross the threshold, there is an expectation that they will be assimilated and behave in concert with the mind of the corporation, like members of *the Borg collective.*

New employees must be able to don the corporate Values Veil without discomfort, which is why the most important tool for building tribes is recruiting for fit. This is a critical ingredient in tribal growth and evolution. The process of induction is the second most important tool in building alignment between the two parts of the person – their outside world and their employment world.

Notes

1 The word 'board' is used to describe those who control the organisation. It may be a single person such as an owner or a group. The common denominator is the ability to exercise power and control.

2 As a general principle, corporations are recognized as legal entities separate from their shareholders, officers and directors. Corporate obligations remain the liability of the entity and not of the shareholders, directors or officers who own and/or act for the entity. However, the law of corporate criminal responsibility and personal liability of the guiding minds is rapidly evolving, creating exceptions to the corporate veil in recognition that the corporation's actions are a function of the people of the corporation.

3 Individuals are liable for criminal acts, even if done in the name of the corporation – e.g. murder, fraud or for their personal motives such as fraud or theft.

4 A new book, *How, Maximising Top Down and Bottom Up Communication*, will detail developments in the field.

5 Laws to combat financial crimes such as money laundering, tax evasion, financing of terrorism and corruption require additional due diligence. Dealing with a black-listed person, commodity or in US$ is used by the US Department of Justice to claim jurisdiction.

6 Mehrabian, A., and Ferris, S. R. (1967). Inference of attitudes from nonverbal communication in two channels. *Journal of Consulting Psychology,* 31(3), 248–252.

7 Which will be explained in detail in *How* to be published in 2018.

8 These were practices of the Eskimo and Hopi Indians.

7 The role of corporate values

> **Key points:**
>
> **Multiple sets of values operate inside organisations:**
>
> - Formal values set out in codes, principles and belief statements;
> - The real operating values;
> - The values that each person brings with them;
> - The values of each country of operation.
>
> **The effectiveness of the formal values is determined by:**
>
> - Whether the values are lived and enforced by leaders;
> - The role adherence to the values plays in determining reward.
>
> **To be effective values need to:**
>
> - Be simple and easily understood;
> - Be difficult to reinterpret to find gaps to justify bad behaviour;
> - Be universal;
> - Address the primal drivers of fear, safety, trust, leadership, followship, belonging and altruism.
>
> **Harm and the Harm Principles meet the effectiveness criteria**

Business ethics is an oxymoron.

Like any popularised generalisation, there may be some truth in the above but it is not universal. However, it is not the truth that matters – it is the perception. The dilemma for corporations is that the huge investment in values programmes is not yielding the hoped-for returns.Every corporation, in fact every group, has

The role of corporate values   127

values expressed in one form or another, whether formally published, or just 'known'. An examination of corporate websites reveals examples of behavioural prescriptions. Very quickly you will notice a wide range of behaviours grouped under headings such as values, ethics, principles and codes. There will also be a plethora of policies, standards and procedures.

Corporations expect employees to behave ethically, adhere to the published principles and codes and live the values. Blah! Add goals, targets, performance measures, balanced score cards, policies, procedures and processes, and the average employee could be forgiven for not knowing where to start and which behavioural drivers take precedence for the good of the corporation. There is no rigour and little logic.

Considerable effort and cost will have been expended in making sure the published set of values[1] scans well, and looks fantastic in published documents, posters, screen savers and embossed plaques. This perfectly polished set of behaviours and standards will have been formally endorsed by the board as an expression of their behavioural priorities. Cynics, however, would say that the values are what the board believes investors, regulators, potential recruits and the community expects.

Cynicism aside, the quality test for values is not the lustre and polish. The real tests are:

- Are the values simple to understand and intuitive to implement?
- Do the values require employees to sublimate their personal real-world values in favour of the values of the corporation?
- Are the values actually lived – top down?

7.1 The lack of real meaning

Values statements usually have a self-evident goodness, but too often lack clarity of meaning. They describe the universal picture, but not in the detail needed by an employee working in a foreign outpost, and/or ten layers away from the board. Values are typically broad, which leaves them open to misinterpretation. Words and phrases like *honest, act with integrity* and *customer focussed* are self-evidently good, but what do they mean to the employee?

In practice, these wonder words are qualified and limited. For example, 'we are open and transparent[2] in our communications', is *prima facie* a good thing, but the first question asked by employees is 'how open?' What corporate secrets are never to be disclosed? What data is confidential to the client? What about salary? How much do we hold back, hoping the customer will never ask? Is being open the same as making full disclosure – warts and all!

The sales process is commonly filled with hyperbole, sometimes mis-statements, and the supporting documentation is too often opaque, filled with lengthy language, devised by lawyers, to protect the corporation. The minute size of print used for the terms and conditions is often not even legible. If one is being

128 *Harm and the corporation*

generous, the unintended consequence is that the sales process is anything but transparent.

Typically, an employee, wanting to behave correctly, seeks clarification of what a value means in a specific work situation. Many will be fobbed off by their manager, who is unwilling to commit. The employees are told, 'use their common sense', whatever that means. After breaches flowing from too little, or too much, openness, a hodgepodge of clarifications and qualifications will be added. Exceptions will be enumerated.

To solve the problem of ambiguity, explanatory codes are developed. Codes tend to cover specific situations, with enumerated examples illustrating the required responses. Yet for every situation enumerated, there will be dozens left out and open to interpretation. 'Does this code apply?' 'Is there a gap?' It is impossible to build a comprehensive set of values using loaded language that requires contextual interpretation.

In parallel, corporations develop policies and procedures. These are carefully crafted, hyper-detailed, legally reviewed and rarely short. In one company, the printed stack was more than 3 metres high, and those were just for compliance, issued by the three corporate layers – head office, division and country. Sitting at the end of the chain, employees could be forgiven for not knowing what was required, even if they had read it all.

What is the corporate response to lack of understanding? More training and intensified communications.

Communications departments of large multi-nationals insist that the text, form and substance of values be enshrined in the official corporate language, using the designated font, colour and format. Everything is cast in immutable stone. They adhere to an idea that having a uniform approach is critical to success in creating a uniform set of behaviours. This is at best naïve and is patently incorrect in globalised corporations. Language, culture, form, learning style and authority/leadership/followship models differ, so why assume one size suits all?

The corporate response to a breach of values is like watching a local talking to a foreigner without the language skills. When the local is not understood, he simply repeats the statements louder and more slowly. The corporate equivalent is to publish their requirements more frequently on different channels, in parallel with mandated e-learning courses.

The outcome is saturation. The messages become noise. Staff boast how quickly they got through the course – often by tapping the space bar and guessing the answers – not how much they learnt, or what it meant for them. Compliance training is 'sheep dipping'.

Too often, the assessment of values programmes focuses on easily measurable and relatively useless data points that can be used to satisfy regulators. Typical measures include:

- Did the senior executives including the Board formally adopt/endorse the values?
- Was there consistent and pervasive communication?

- Was the course content appropriate?
- Did people attend?
- Did attendees know and understand the content?

The programme is then deemed successful because the target number of employees received the message and attended training and scored above a threshold in the multiple guess quiz. It is not just the fault of compliance, or the internal communications teams. Management has to take responsibility, but they too are poorly equipped. They complain about the time and cost and the lack of change, yet every year the cycle is repeated, but as Einstein said:

> Insanity is doing the same thing over and over again, expecting a different result.

It does not work, yet it is repeated, not in the real belief that it will magically become effective and change behaviour, but to set up a regulatory defence that 'we did everything reasonably possible'.

By themselves, the measures above tell you nothing about how the organisation behaves. It simply says values were published and communicated, and staff were made aware and understood the values, as measured by multiple-choice questions and answers. On these measures, ENRON would have been awarded a gold star.

More useful measures, albeit more difficult to obtain and interpret, are surveys and feedback that examine perceived behaviours and attitude, not knowledge. These measures provide a clearer, though not perfect, picture of what is really going on. There is a huge difference in being able to say '100% of staff understood that there is a value called transparency' and 'the degree to which staff say they believe/feel transparency happens in various communications, for example: with customers; top down; within the teams; and across silos'.

The problem is that we measure the easily measurable, not what needs to be measured, or what provides real insight into the effectivenss of training and communications. For leaders to engender followship requires a different approach. A novel process, the Engagement Cascade™, is set out in the companion publication, *How?*, scheduled for publication in mid-2019.

7.2 Contextual interpretation

Even if the meaning of the corporate values is clear, we established in Chapter 2 that what constitutes acceptable behaviour is contextual. Judgement of right and wrong, good and bad depends on whose values are being employed, when the judgement was made, where the actions took place and what were the specifics of the situation.

Meaning and intent are lost when the language is susceptible to contextual interpretation. Having open and honest communication, being full and frank, clear and concise are ambiguous phrases even before the cultural and contextual

130 *Harm and the corporation*

nuances are introduced. What is open in one country may be seen as rude in another. The Dutch pride themselves on being straightforward, an admirable trait that can cause great offence, say for the Japanese, who may have been expecting a subtler style.

Where the meaning is unambiguous, local practice can often introduce conflict. How do you explain a corporate policy banning bribery, or nepotism, or favouring friends, when it is part of the everyday culture of that market place? The process of understanding the intent behind the value needs to engage at the cultural level, even though this may be deemed politically incorrect and insensitive.

Where there is a genuine conflict of values – bribery being a classic example – the language of right and wrong does not resonate. Your wrong is my right! Your bad is my good. Your prohibition is my essential. What language needs to be deployed to get a different result? Without constructive dialogue and discussion, little will change. This is the bedrock on which the success of the Engagement Cascade™ is founded. Constructive discussion of the issue, utilising the language of harm, diminishes the power of cultural differences.

7.3 Finding the gap

Within the corporation, the pursuit of the gap is alive and well. Managers look for ways to justify a course of action. They explore loopholes and interpretations of the various formal values and control systems, rarely asking the question, what was the real intent? They don't ask, because the answer may be inconvenient.

Finding the gaps gets rewarded – at least in the short term.

A culture of finding the gaps, while legal, can be harmful because it is pernicious. It sends a message to employees about how rules are to be approached. *This is how we do things around here!* Finding gaps is cloaked in logic, reason and the respectability of legalistic construction. As soon as a behavioural prescription is written, someone will parse it. They will shape its implementation, ignoring or subverting the intent, in order to justify acting in a way the powers that be had prohibited and thought had been eliminated.

The consequence is a culture which believes that if it is not illegal, or specifically proscribed, then it is OK even if it is harmful. The potential impact of the reinterpretation of meaning, whether through cultural parsing, ambiguity or the exploitation of gaps, is crystallised by the power of the local manager. The consequence is that the corporate approved values and behaviours are lost, replaced by local interpretations that favour the manager's bias, priorities, expediency or goals.

Employee allegiance will be to the local alpha manager, who has the power to dictate *what the values really mean for us*. The result is disengagement from the corporate message. Alignment is transferred to the local values and over time the

The role of corporate values   131

unit culture coalesces around the localised values, which can persist even after the manager has departed.

The REAL way we do things round here is then perpetuated by the informal social forces of peers, folklore and myth, illustrated with examples, woven into stories told over coffee, the water cooler or over a drink.

What is an employee to think? How is the employee expected to act?

7.4 Failure of corporate and market values

There is only one ethic in business – to make money.

ENRON – a blueprint for future failures

In 2000 ENRON published a set of well-respected values. They were highly visible. They were prominent in reception, on every floor and in all publications. The values were communicated vigorously, yet failed to stem the criminal corporate behaviour.
ENRON's Published Values

Communication

We have an obligation to communicate. Here, we take the time to talk with one another . . . and to listen. We believe that information is meant to move and that information moves people.

Reality: In practice, the communication was used to hype and disguise. The information communicated was often false. People felt communicated with, but . . .

Respect

We treat others as we would like to be treated ourselves. We do not tolerate abusive or disrespectful treatment.

Reality: Lying to staff was common and is the epitome of disrespect. Those who disagreed with the leadership were quickly marginalised. There was no respect for difference of opinion. Respect was a veneer of civility.

Integrity

We work with customers and prospects openly, honestly and sincerely. When we say we will do something, we will do it; when we say we cannot or will not do something, then we won't do it.

Reality: Deception, dishonesty, prevarication and manipulation of the facts was the norm.

132 *Harm and the corporation*

Excellence

> We are satisfied with nothing less than the very best in everything we do. We will continue to raise the bar for everyone. The great fun here will be for all of us to discover just how good we can really be.

Reality: The greatest point of excellence was in identifying and exploiting gaps in laws and markets. Arbitrage was the code for exploitation.

ENRON's real values

While never formally published, ENRON had a parallel, supervening set of values and systemic behaviours that included:

- Self-belief to the point of self-delusion as to their infallibility – hubris;
- Silencing of dissent;
- Extreme risk taking to pursue aggressive growth;
- Entrepreneurship not stewardship;
- Shareholder value and bonus generation above all else;
- Bullying;
- Arrogance;
- Dishonesty;
- Irrational loyalty.

Following the collapse, I interviewed a senior ENRON finance executive. I asked her: 'Why, when you knew the figures you provided were inflated by head office so ENRON could make the earnings target, you said nothing, did nothing, but bought more shares while Skilling was selling?' Her answer still resonates with me a decade later and goes to the heart of when the values veil becomes the corporate mask and the individual's internal values systems shut down and are replaced by those of the parasitic collective.

She said: 'I did not want to rock the boat. We were having so much fun.'

Please pass the Kool Aid.[3] This was a classic example of the power of the myth to distort thought processes so that illogical decisions and actions were taken.

The temptation for corporations is to harness the power of the mask to motivate and control employees. But, as ENRON demonstrated, masks encourage distortion of reality, which is ultimately destructive and unsustainable. Great in the short run, but unlikely to survive.

The list of failures of values in the corporate world did not begin or end with ENRON. ENRON was just spectacularly large. In 2008 the financial crisis took effect. The failure of the financial systems can be traced in part to a failure of the markets' values foundations and partly to the unquestioning adherence of those who were subsumed by the market's morality mask. For decades, the market-

The role of corporate values   133

mask-wearing acolytes pontificated that the market would self-correct. The market knows best. Trust the market and deregulate.

The systemic failures and scandals in the finance industry were not because the institutions did not have cogent public values. It is probable that a sub-rosa morality mask was in operation, distorting behaviour. What masks were at play in the 2008 financial crisis?

- Quarterly share performance driven by investor pursuit of alpha;
- Bonus entitlement;
- The 'Market' knows best myth;
- Buyer beware, even if we make it impossible for you to understand and have seduced you into buying with false promises;
- If it's legal, then do it.

The power of the morality masks worn by some finance executives was so great that those interviewed felt they had done nothing wrong. In a finance industry workshop I was running in New York a few months after the Lehman Bros collapse, the first question asked was not about the future, but about the security of their annual bonuses! They argued that they had not broken the law. They had a contractual right, so why should they give up their bonuses? There was no acceptance of responsibility, no contrition – personal or collective. Very few finance executives ever paraded on the public contrition catwalk. Fewer have been held accountable. There has been some regulation, but underneath, not much has changed.
Why?

There is not enough pressure to force change. The public may clamour, groups like Occupy Wall Street may protest, but the underlying structure has not changed. We have new complex laws and regulations, but they often do not go to the root cause. When we do get legislation that can be enforced, there is not enough political will to support prosecution. There is a belief that the politicians are owned by, or if not owned by, influenced to not attack, industry – finance, military, auto, pharma, legal. There is a self-serving symbiosis which is being railed against by the public who voted for Trump. 'Why are there so few white-collar perpetrators of the financial crisis and economic and social destruction in prison?' is a question asked by many.

Our whole financial system is an artificial construct. We have mythologised unchallengeable elements such as the power and self-correcting nature of the market. We developed theories of trickle down, supply side economics to justify models of behaviour. We demonise government debt, except when it props us up. We stand in awe of the power of the financial markets. We are overjoyed by rises, dismayed by falls, believing that, like chicken entrails, they portend the future. And we act on these irrational fears and hopes in our mythical market world, giving substance to unreality.

Do the rises and falls really presage the future? Are they real measures of the health of a company, a sector, the local economy and the world? Sometimes. Bubbles inflate and we rejoice. Bubbles collapse and we wring our hands.

134 *Harm and the corporation*

Sometimes market movements are cynical reflections of manipulated trading sentiments that are exploited by those who can. Gambling up or down, making reality from the myth.

The operation of *the market* and the behaviour of the players who really control the market are a long way from the foundations that once drove corporate behaviour – a clear link between ownership, management and purpose. Corporations today pursue profit and growth in share price for investors, but in a market that operates in a mythical paradigm.

The market myth and its power to influence our reality is important, because it is a useful example of the power of the myth as an instrument of social control. The market myth drives behaviours that coalesce in a tangible culture and it is culture that truly drives corporate behaviour – not just knowledge of values, rules, policies and procedures.

Notes

1 For simplicity, I have chosen the word 'values' as the collective when discussing generic behavioural constructs. It is arbitrary. Words like ethics, principles, codes, etc. could all have been used.
2 Two billion references in a Google search including government and corporations.
3 In 1978, 913 members of the People's Temple cult committed suicide by drinking grape-flavoured, cyanide laced Kool-Aid. Prior to the mass suicide, Jim Jones, the cult leader, had conducted suicide drills where people would line up to receive dummy fatal drinks. This establishes that at least the adults knew they would die by drinking the Kool Aid.

8 Culture is critical

> **Key points:**
>
> **Culture is the catch-all to describe how an organisation behaves, which reflects its underlying beliefs, attitudes and lived values.**
>
> *A strong positive culture:*
>
> - Reduces the need for controls and supervision;
> - Aligns performance and norms and restricting outlier behaviour;
> - Reduces the impact of silos;
> - Increases engagement.
>
> **Negative cultures reduce the effectiveness of controls and increase risk.**
>
> **Culture is difficult to measure, but there are visible indicators to diagnose dysfunctional cultures.**

The work culture is the differentiating force that changes a worker from someone who just turns up for work to a valuable employee, who engages and makes things happen. Culture is the fulcrum that leverages performance and aligns behaviours. A positive culture allows a corporation to operate with fewer controls, fewer rules, fewer policies and less internal policing. It is cheaper. A negative culture destroys value, increases risk and decreases effective top-down control.

Steve Jobs' transformation of Apple was driven by the culture he created.[1] It permeated every cell of Apple – from product inception, marketing and packaging to the retail process and even the architecture of the store. Without the culture, his vision may never have blossomed. His second phase of Apple leadership, post Pixar, was a very different cultural environment from that in his first incarnation. There was less fear and abuse, more vision, more pursuit of excellence, wrapped in a story with the customer at its core. He created an Apple myth that everyone could believe in – staff, customers, suppliers and the stock

136 *Harm and the corporation*

market. The Jobs personal myth enabled his vision and standards to be known and feared in every crevice of the company. Everyone knew what was expected every day from everyone and it was NOT written down.

Creating and maintaining an *appropriate* culture enables corporations, regardless of industry, maturity, size or location, to operate efficiently and effectively, minimising cost and maximising performance. Without enabling behaviours, it is impossible to maximise results, notwithstanding having the best strategy, opportunity, people, products and resources. No amount of capital, political connection, networks and inventions are sufficient by themselves.

8.1 What is corporate culture?

Culture is simply *'the way we do things round here.'* It is a function of the organisation's lived values, made tangible through the visible behaviours and expressed attitudes of its constituent members.

Schein conceptualised culture as a series of layers, like an onion. The outer rings are more visible. His outer visible rings consist of artefacts such as colours, logos, uniforms and dress codes, slogans, look, feel, the weapons and tools – smarter phones, slimmer notebooks, bigger offices, platinum credit cards, embossed cards. These are the traditional easy-to-implement symbols. They say a lot, but are not sufficient.

The other visible layer is the exhibited behaviours. Colleagues and customers can see and observe these behaviours, of which there are many components. The next layer is less visible. These are the norms of the organisation. What is expected. These are harder to assess. They require subjective description, which lays them open to distortion. While we can watch behaviours, and emulate them, the norms are inferred. Ideally, understanding the norms is by discussion and communication. But unlike the next layer, the corporation's formal values, norms are rarely fully codified.

Values in the Schein model are not just what is written, but what is lived. As we have seen, ENRON had two sets of values – the publicly declared and the real. It is the real, invisible, values that shape culture. The existence of multiple sets of values, like in ENRON, is indicative of potential dysfunction.

The core of Schein's model is what people really believe. Beneath the norms and the corporation's values, at the very heart are the real beliefs and myths. These are rarely discussed. In a fear-driven, dysfunctional culture where expressing one's beliefs, especially doubts, is construed as disloyalty or subversion, they are never declared – not if you want to survive. The norms must be internalised if you want to thrive.

It would be wrong to think that there can only be one uniform, homogenous culture. Every industry has a culture and every organisation within that industry will be different. Within an organisation each location and even department will have its own version of the organisation's culture. The way the office works in India will not be the same as in Peru, USA, Australia or Europe. The accountants will not have the same culture as the designers, or marketers, who may not align

Culture is critical 137

with sales. IT is different to audit and no one aligns or identifies with compliance, except perhaps risk. Functional cultural difference is common across the entire spectrum of organisations: corporate, private, public, charitable, for profit, social, commercial, military and law enforcement.

Minor differences are not harmful, providing there is complete alignment to the corporation's core values, central beliefs and purpose.

Cultural cohesion is independent of the particular set of values. A strong, cohesive, high-trust and enabling culture can develop regardless of the particular values, beliefs and purpose. A drug-dealing, gun-running biker gang will have a culture, defined by its values, principles and codes and realised in behaviours and devotion to code, as powerful as the most dedicated Special Forces military unit or evangelical church. They will align themselves by adopting dress, totems and symbols. They will define themselves by adopting the required language and mode of speech, greetings and patterns of behaviour. The expectations of the gang will be understood and socialised, and breaches dealt with.

Each tribe has its unique values and myths that are believed by the members. So does ISIL. While we may despise the actions of terrorist groups such as ISIL, they have values, principles, ideas and myths that shaped their culture and determined their actions. They have a myth that binds them. Their myth was developed and is perpetuated, not in written constitutions, but through emotion-fuelled stories told in graphic HD colour that pander to the most primitive parts of being human.

It is wrong to say gangs, terrorists and groups we dislike, or fear, have no values. To do so makes it impossible to understand them. What we must do is recognise that they have values we abhor, which is the reciprocal of how they feel about us.

Values alone are rarely effective in achieving unity, or singularity of culture. As discussed previously, values are easily morphed to fit local context, whether inside a corporation or in broader society.[2] At each layer, across divisions and within each silo, leaders and managers redefine the values, applying a local flavour – redefining some, selectively applying others and adding new values of their own. Rarely are these changes written, for to do so would incur the wrath of the corporate *values' guardians*.

Pixar, the engine of Steve Jobs' fortune, did not succeed because of its specialised technology, although that was the main reason Jobs purchased the company, but because of the single unified culture of the creative team led by John Lattimer and Ed Cattermole.[3] His time at Pixar changed Jobs, particularly his thinking on the role of story in shaping beliefs and building culture.

Alignment with purpose alone will not build a cohesive culture. Public hospitals exist to provide health services. Their values statements will be laudable proclamations; for example, the delivery of quality medical services, something all staff can identify with. But Western hospital cultures are not renowned for their allegiance to health care above all else. Hospitals are infamously siloed, replete with stratified sub-structures, despite the dedication of individual staff. This culture is demotivating, decreasing engagement with a loss of efficiency and effectiveness.

138   *Harm and the corporation*

Hospitals are too often riven by belief systems around status, hierarchy and power – the white-coated gods – that diminish the power of the published values. Compare this to the esprit de corps of hospitals in emergency zones like Aleppo, or Médicins sans Frontières, where miracles are performed despite limited resources. The volunteer emergency hospitals are populated by those who share a dream, a vision – a self-styled myth that unifies them. Their culture is different from that of the pristine, sanitised security of the well-established and well-funded hospitals.

8.2 The dark side of culture

Not everything about cultures is beneficial. Cultures, if allowed to proliferate, differentiate and metastasise, will breed reinforced silo loyalties. Silos breed inefficiency. Communication is slowed, filtered and distorted. Delay and uncertainty increases. Trust beyond the immediate silo and team decreases. When assistance is sought, it is given grudgingly and rarely volunteered. *We mind our own business. Their problem is not our fault and their failure may be our gain.* Powerful leaders, sitting at the top of silos, often use the language of 'them and us' accompanied by a sub-culture of subtle intimidation.

A culture of fanatical blind adherence to a set of values (the morality mask) is dangerous and is not advocated as a model for corporations, particularly if the dominant value is profit and bonus above all else. The profit mask, like the hate mask, can produce spectacular short-term results. But masks generate risks of blind adherence with no thought of consequences.

Fear-based cultures might work in violent organisations, but in our mainstream corporate world, where building customer and market trust is critical, fear will be counterproductive. Fear to speak up, fear of reprisal, fear of failure, fear of being wrong, fear of making mistakes. Fear destroys communication and identification and the sharing of problems before they become large.

A fearful culture breeds cover-up and inhibits creativity, problem solving and progress. Fear promotes group-think and avoidance of divergence. Fear destroys trust and inhibits the development of good ideas. Fear may breed reluctant obedience, but that is not a substitute for a positive culture. Worst of all, a fear-based culture does not promote positive interactions with customers, suppliers and the market place.

The absence of fear as a tool of control should not be confused with a lack of discipline. A disciplined adherence to the agreed values is essential, as is an even-handed enforcement of breaches of the values.

8.3 From values lived to the corporate morality mask

In Chapter 2.2 we introduced a continuum of adherence to values. At one end of the spectrum, individuals maintained their own set of values and ignored those of the society in which they operated. At the other end of the spectrum is the morality mask, where the individual's values are sublimated entirely to those of

Culture is critical 139

the new group and all behaviours align absolutely with those required by the group.

In the middle, more common situation, people moved from one group to another, donning and doffing the Values Veils, adopting the practices and behaviours and implicitly the values of each new group.

They could do this because the differences in values and behavioural expectations were compatible. In each transition, the person took on a veil with the new, but complementary, values. The required changes in behaviour were subtle and not conflicting, often revolving around language, non-verbal communication and focus of discussion and action.

The wearing of a morality mask is most visible in anti-social organisations. Here we see the total blind adherence to the group's values: extreme loyalty, violence, intimidation, use of slogans and symbols. There are distinguishing features that provide latch points of identity. Whether it is the colours of a bike gang, a military death squad, or blind extreme political rallies, the characteristics are visible. No one challenges. Everyone obeys. Dissent is shut down. Dissenters are dealt with.

In the corporate world, the morality mask is subtler, blending into the norm. The corporate pirates do not wear eye patches, carry swords and yell 'Avast'. Their weapons are those of the everyday – spreadsheets, contracts, financing. Many of the values required by the corporate morality mask have been enshrined into the myth of our social consciousness. We admire loyalty, hard work, profitability, growth, income, team spirit. We measure individual success by power, wealth, possessions. We judge by the cut of the suit, the quality of the cloth, the brand of watch, pen and car, where we live, the clubs we join, the galleries we frequent, the crowd we run with.

One of the problem with traditional values-based behaviour alignment systems is the lack of guidelines to limit aberrant behaviour. Individual values can be pushed to an extreme. Loyalty is good until it becomes blind followship. Profit and winning are good, but at what cost? Sales success without caring about impact of selling the customer what they did not need or understand should not be regarded as success. We have no generally agreed norms about when enough is enough.

In the case study discussed earlier, the division had an extremely strong identity. Unfortunately, they not only created a myth that their superior performance flowed from their unique identity but also an unchallengeable belief set that they knew better than the rest of the corporation. Their standard defence was, 'they don't understand'. Followed by, 'Leave us alone and we will grow and make profit. We will grow the brand and this will benefit you.'

All this was true – until their avoidable failure. Avoidable if the corporate processes had been followed. If advice had been heeded. If their systems had been transparent to oversight. Their behaviour exhibited many mask-like properties, albeit with good motives.

Masks empower the self-righteous and can distort and sublimate internal systems of control.

140 *Harm and the corporation*

8.4 The Jekyll and Hyde syndrome

One of the questions that has perplexed and intrigued society and psychologists, sociologists and behaviourists is why individuals, who are good with their family and friends, can do bad things in their job. Why do good people follow orders of authority figures?[4] What happens from the time when they leave home to when they cross the corporate portal to their office? What triggers the transformation from Jekyll to Hyde?[5] Do they have two morality masks and become different people? Or does the organisational mask – corporate, military or gang – embody such apparent duality?

- Why does the bank helpline officer, who demanded, and got, great service from the coffee chain, not offer the same level of service to callers?
- Why does the executive who demanded honesty and full disclosure from the stay-out-late teen, submit marketing material that shades the truth and omits vital information?
- Why does the righteous preacher have affairs?
- How can a concentration camp guard kiss his child goodbye and then do unspeakable things to children of 'the others'?

Masks enable duality, or even multiplicity of seemingly inconsistent behaviours. Violent gangs protect their family, often enshrining in their codes family values that are not dissimilar to those of the natural world.

The difficulty for each of us is to find the balance between loyalty and blind followship; following orders, but speaking up without fear when the orders are wrong; keeping business confidential, but blowing the whistle (internally first) when actions are wrong; being able to question, say no, raise issues and make suggestions without fear.

Knowledge and understanding of consequence are of themselves no predictor of behaviour. People smoke, knowing the link to cancer; overeat, knowing the problems of obesity; drive fast, knowing the correlation of speed, accident and severity of injury. Key ENRON executives knowingly committed personal financial suicide and perpetrated directly, or through omission, or silence, a crime on staff and society at large. Yet they were otherwise good, sane people. Given this ability to ignore deferred risk and consequence, it is understandable why the powerful forces unleashed by the morality mask have the power to turn off the internal values. While the mask is in place, the fusion is complete.

Preventing masks requires a balance in the choice of behaviours and lived values.

8.5 Indicators of a dysfunctional culture

Research into corruption and the various banking scandals has identified behavioural and structural indicators that do not show up in compliance, risk management and internal audit reviews that rarely focus on culture. The standard procedure, process and activity evaluations may identify issues perpetrated by individuals and groups, but rarely pinpoint systemic top-down practices.

The indicators are organised into seven groups. You will note some thematic overlap across language used, drivers, structure and individual characteristics. This reflects the complexity of the corporate world and the imprecise art employed in diagnosing and analysing behaviour and culture. By understanding the relative importance of each of the factors set out, it is possible to develop a cultural risk matrix. Each of these factors will be present to varying degrees in every organisation, including ones with a healthy trustworthy culture. What is critical is to determine the mix and relative dominance of each factor.

1. Growth Imperative

Growth and profitability are key corporate drivers. Problems occur when the pressure for growth outweighs other considerations. The following list of behaviours and mindset are red flags, indicative of the potential distortion of the culture by the growth imperative:

- Belief that the ends justify the means;
- Exaggeration of the importance of goals and targets;
- Pursuit of market dominance;
- Exaggerated focus on the need to win;
- Profitability and sales targets are the dominant performance indicators;
- Sales staff lionised;
- Unrelenting sense of urgency.

2. Leadership behaviours

- Arrogance;
- Autocratic command and control;
- Complacency;
- Denigration of 2nd and 3rd line functions such as compliance, risk, legal and audit;
- Encouragement of 'stretching' the truth in marketing and reporting;
- Implicitly or explicitly justifying the means by stressing the 'end';
- Inducing fear;
- Finding the gaps to allow actions that should not be allowed (policy, law, business principles);
- Fostering internal competition rather than cooperation;
- Ignoring advice;
- Failing to give clear instructions;
- Failing to consult;
- Poor information flow;
- Strict enforcement of hierarchy and channel flow;
- Short-term emphasis over long-term;

142 *Harm and the corporation*

- Silencing opposition and dissent;
- Setting unrealistic targets;
- Decisions and authority cannot be questioned.

3. Organisational Structure

- Collective ownership;
- Complexity of divisions;
- Complexity of functions;
- Complexity of layers;
- Hero teams lightly managed;
- Multiple countries and jurisdictions;
- Poor post-acquisition integration;
- Poor responsibility and accountability;
- Silo-first mindset over inter-silo cooperation;
- Tick boxes to show compliance with systems and processes.

4. Information flow characteristics

- Bad news is suppressed or filtered;
- Success beyond expectations/reason unexamined;
- Flagged problems ignored and those who raise problems pressured to remain silent;
- Suggestions for improvement ignored or denigrated.

5. Performance Management System

- Cost control rewarded without strategic capacity balance;
- Values not part of the balanced score card (how);
- Sales/growth target primary reward trigger;
- Veneration of high flyers – special perks.

6. Norms and the sub-rosa Culture

- Absolute loyalty;
- Aggression when questioned;
- Code of silence;
- Fear;
- Insecurity;
- Low organisational pride but high team pride;
- Low transparency;
- Opaque;
- Powerlessness of the ordinary employee;
- Promotion of rivalry;
- Secrecy.

7. Language

The language used by teams provides a clue to underlying attitudes towards compliance, adherence to values and the broader relationships with customers and the community.

- Adoration of the successful hero;
- Battle metaphors;
- Everyone's doing it;
- Find the gap;
- In-group code to denigrate compliance, values and training;
- It's legal;
- Purpose of company is to make money for shareholders;
- They don't understand local conditions;
- They will never know;
- Us (local team) and them (rest of company).

8.6 Getting the data

There is no simple way to secure the data to evaluate cultural distortion. Four tools have proven useful:

- Anonymous survey tools – overcome fear and reluctance to speak out, but requires trust that identity will be protected. Some cultures mistrust surveys. Some teams will say what is expected.
- Exercises embedded in a broader workshop where the purpose is disguised.
- Anonymous voting in workshops.
- Personal interaction – walking around, individual discussion and interviews.

8.7 The value and costs of engagement

Engagement was first coined by William Kahn in 1990 to describe the way employees related to an organisation – physically, mentally and emotionally. Mind, body and soul. His theory postulated that the higher the level of connection on each of the dimensions, the higher the productivity. Happy, satisfied employees perform better. They don't spend time complaining, taking breaks or looking for new jobs. They don't undermine and, conversely, may actively promote the company to friends as a place to work and do business. The ideas behind engagement are not new. The military use the term morale. Commitment was a popular term in the early 2000s.

There is no agreement on exactly what engagement is, how to measure it and, most importantly, how to create it. If one ignores the differences in approach by firms promoting their particular assessment tool, there are several threads that align with the core behavioural drivers of fear, trust, belonging, leadership and

144 *Harm and the corporation*

role. There is also a cognitive element of alignment with values, a belief in the future (stability, promotion) and the purpose of the organisation.

A non-exhaustive list of factors that contribute to engagement include:

- Effective communications;
- Alignment with values and norms;
- Interpersonal relationship with colleagues (tribe);
- Two-way feedback with manager (proximate alpha leader);
- A belief in a positive future – promotion and increased income (survival);
- Clarity of role and freedom to perform (tools, authority);
- Sense of contributing and being valued.

For want of an agreed technical definition, the idea of engagement could be described as the spirit or ethos of the organisation which excites and motivates people to do the best they can at work. Engagement has many similarities with tribal cohesion.

Regardless of the imprecision in definition, research on the impact of disengagement has revealed:

- Tower Perrins' 2006 global survey[6] found that companies with highly engaged employees had a near 52 per cent lead in performance improvement in operating income, compared with companies whose employees had low engagement scores.
- Companies with high levels of employee engagement improved 19.2 per cent in operating income while companies with low levels of employee engagement declined 32.7 per cent over the study period.
- Engaged employees in the UK take an average of 2.69 sick days per year; the disengaged take 6.192 sick days.
- The CBI reported that sickness absence costs the UK economy £13.4bn a year.
- 70 per cent of engaged employees indicate they have a good understanding of how to meet customer needs; only 17 per cent of non-engaged employees say the same.
- Engaged employees are 87 per cent less likely to leave the organisation than the disengaged.
- 78 per cent of engaged employees would recommend their company's products or services, against 13 per cent of the disengaged.
- Companies with both highly aligned cultures and highly aligned innovation strategies have 17 per cent higher profit growth than companies with low degrees of alignment.
- Gallup says that American companies lose approximately $300 billion in productivity per year due to lack of engagement.
- Companies with engaged workforces perform up to 202 per cent better.
- Of the 70 per cent of American workers who are not reaching their full potential, 52 per cent are not engaged, and another 18 per cent are actively

disengaged. These employees are emotionally disconnected from their companies and may actually be working against their employers' interests; they are less productive, are more likely to steal from their companies, negatively influence their co-workers, miss workdays and drive customers away.
- Gallup estimates that actively disengaged employees cost the USA $450 billion to $550 billion in lost productivity per year.
- 82 per cent of employees are motivated by performance recognition, according to the National Business Research Institute.

8.8 Leadership triggers of disengagement

Once the basic hygiene factors are in place – role, tools, purpose, work space, salary, work contract, health and safety etc. – the key remaining factors are the behaviours of the leaders and the alignment of purpose and values. As discussed earlier, the organisation's purpose and values set is irrelevant. What is critical is that the individual's values – professed and lived – align with the purpose of the organisation and that the members of the organisation can adopt the values without dissonance. Thus, the bike gang, terrorists and criminal enterprises, while having different values, may have high engagement, albeit for anti-social purposes.

Many of the indicators of a dysfunctional culture are also factors in disengagement. While the research is yet to be carried out in a systematic way, there appears to be a correlation between dysfunctional leadership indicators and poor engagement.

What is clear is that certain managerial personality types, tagged the cluster B disorders, have behaviours that destroy engagement. They exploit team members rather than keep them safe. They bully to produce performance and exhibit extremes of favouritism and disapproval. Unfortunately, they are also the highly driven, target-oriented sales producers so highly prized and admired.

Notes

1 *Insight to Genius – Steve Jobs' Handbook*, 2014, Mike Lotzof.
2 See Chapter 2.2.
3 Jobs purchased Pixar not to make animated movies, but to use the technology for medical and defence image processing. Lattimer convinced Jobs to not fire the animation team.
4 Research was undertaken (and since replicated by others) by Stanley Milgram in 1963 and published in 1963. *Journal of Abnormal and Social Psychology*, 67, 371–378.
5 *The Strange Case of Dr Jekyll and Mr Hyde* by R L Stevenson. 1886.
6 Willis Tower Perrins, 2017 Global Nefits Attitude Survey, www.willistowerswatson. com/en/insights/2017/11/2017-global-benefits-attitudes-survey.

9 The value of 'do no harm' in changing your organisation

Key points:

- Preventing harm and being perceived as reducing harm are the foundations for building internal and external trust. Harm plays to the primal fear driver as well as our rational self.
- Harm and the Harm Principles are simple, easy to understand and can be applied by everyone in every organisation with a minimal amount of training and communication.
- The idea of making decisions to avoid legal but harmful actions is easy for staff to understand and apply because harm aligns with our primary emotional fear driver.
- Doing harm is clear and unambiguous and cannot easily be parsed to justify bad behaviour. There are no gaps to be found and exploited.
- The idea of harm is new, which makes it an interesting topic for formal and informal communications.
- Making the avoidance of harm a core value empowers staff to question and challenge potentially harmful decisions and actions which may have been justified because they were legal.
- Harm reduction is a more concrete and relatable way to describe the purpose of corporate social responsibility activities.

The current approach to behaviour change fails to yield a return on investment. Billions are wasted on ineffectual compliance, ethics education and communications programmes. Bad things continue to happen at an alarming frequency. Unacceptably risky behaviour continues. Trust dissipates. Staff engagement remains stubbornly low.

9.1 Why then is harm different?

1. Simplicity

- Corporations only need to apply the first principle – *Do no Harm*.
- The construct *Legal but Harmful* is easy to understand and relate to.

In workshops carried out in over sixty countries, when staff were asked *'what harms could flow from your work?'*, all staff, regardless of level, industry or country, could quickly identify the harms that could flow from the work they did. The concept took minutes to deliver.

The application of the concept to their own world flowed seamlessly. Critically, the individual and collective insights were actionable. Not only did they know what was wrong, but they could develop ways to fix it.

Do no harm aligns with, but is different from, the Google injunction *'don't be evil'*. The difference is that the meaning of evil is morally and contextually dependent, like right and wrong. Harm is not. Harm is an empirically determinable outcome that is independent of culture or context.

I have had passionate advocates insisting that the sixth principle – **Reduce Harm** – is vital. I agree that it is important, but it is not critical. If nothing else, being seen as not doing harm is the essential foundation for rebuilding trust because it reduces fears and concerns. Actively reducing harm not of your own making is the bonus play.

2. Emotional alignment

Inflicting harm gives pleasure to psychopaths and sociopaths and is justified by those operating under a code where inflicting harm on others is justified by a set of beliefs, whether religious, social or financial. Reckless infliction of harm in pursuit of profit is part of the public stereotype of Wall Street and financiers. Like every stereotype it is not universal, but the perceptions live.

Having the right not to be harmed is at the core of how people value themselves.

Being comfortable inflicting harm as part of the ordinary course of business is not the profile of the ideal employee, leader or corporation. Inflicting harm, without a justification such as self-defence, conflicts with most people's personal values.

A corporate statement – do no harm – resonates and aligns with the kind of people most organisations want to employ. One of the greatest barriers to making values statements a way of life for employees is the dissonance caused, whether through language or content, by differences between corporate values and those of each member of staff.

There is no point of dissonance with the injunction to ***Do No Harm!***

148 *Harm and the corporation*

3. *Clarity of meaning*

The language of harm is simple, intuitive and easy for staff to understand and relate to.

Every prescriptive requirement – whether imposed by a law, internal code or process – can be reframed into the language of harm.

Instead of rote observance, staff understand why! They are empowered. The problem of conflict with local custom and practice is discussed later.

4. *No gaps*

Prescriptive codes are never comprehensive. They invite the pursuit of finding gaps or reframing meaning to justify unacceptable actions.

If staff can identify a harm, even in the absence of an explicit instruction, they can raise an internal flag as to whether the action should be carried out. This reduces risk by raising potential issues.

5. *Awareness that harms can be caused*

One of the greatest barriers to behavioural change is the lack of the real awareness and understanding of the impact of consequences of actions. 'I did not think, know'.

Awareness that harms could flow from actions changes how staff feel about their actions. This operates in both the fact/logic part of the brain and the primitive feeling/emotion zone. It is no longer an abstraction.

6. *Newness*

Harm is an ancient concept, but it is new in the corporate lexicon. Staff are inured to the language of ethics, values and law. They roll their eyes, shrug their shoulders and reluctantly attend training.

Harm's very newness creates interest. Staff approach the idea with a curious and open mind. The craving for the new and different provides a rare opportunity to harness the informal communications networks and channel them to operate in parallel with the formal corporate systems, amplifying the message.

Social water-cooler chatter is a powerful force that often undermines the formal messages and enables the perpetuation of sub-rosa values systems. Its power derives from the potency of peer pressure and the way stories and myths are created and perpetuated in the corporate social environment.

Harnessing the informal can only be done by having a new topic that staff want to talk about. The nature of Harm is fertile ground for staff to develop and tell stories that can reinforce and support a robust culture.

The very act of inviting staff to freely voice their concerns in the language of harm may itself become a topic of conversation – both for sceptics and would be believers.

The value of 'do no harm' in changing your organisation   149

7. Change in perspective

Harm provides a different lens through which staff can examine their actions, as well as those of their colleagues, managers and the corporation as a whole. Instead of referring to complex codes of conduct, crafted values statements or legal injunctions, staff can look at an action and ask themselves, '*what if any harm flows?*'.

Breaking the standard funnel approach and empowering staff to 'think differently' will generate new insights and raise issues and risks that were previously unseen or, in some cases, covered up. This may challenge some managers who are happy to ignore harmful consequences in pursuit of growth and profit.

8. Mindful empowerment

Our systemised approach to corporate activity creates a mindset of doing what you are told and following orders, often laid down in detailed procedures and enabled by automated systems. There is a mindlessness that suppresses questioning. There are good reasons to systematise and automate. Errors and risk are reduced. It is more efficient and cost effective.

The risk that flows from slavish, blind adherence to poor procedures and broken processes is the suppression of feedback necessary for continuous improvement. The corporate response to system failure is a knee-jerk reaction, usually involving expensive consultants, blame, anxiety and massive investment in management time, systems changes and, inevitably, more training.

The alternative is a fluid dynamic feedback system.

Empowering staff to identify and raise harms supports a broader mindset of continuous feedback and improvement. It strengthens the culture, reduces risk and increases engagement.

9. A tool for chunking and problem solving

Harm elimination offers a different perspective for problem solving. It provides a way of chunking and categorising big issues into manageable elements. For example, process issues can be broken down to isolate any source of harm. The way marketing material or contract documentation is prepared can be viewed from the perspective of what harm might flow to customers and suppliers if the content is opaque, complex or the font illegible.

Call centres are notorious for scripts, designed for efficiency of call handling rather than customer benefit. Every point of contact with the customer could be re-examined from the perspective of what fears the customer might have. The same is true of communities. Consciously addressing and eliminating the fear of harm is a powerful tool in rebuilding trust.

This does not require a massive investment, or the engagement of sophisticated consultants. It is a process that can and has been built into team meetings at which the staff charged with day-to-day activities are asked for their insights.

150   *Harm and the corporation*

There are few problems inside corporations that have not been identified internally and for which staff have not considered solutions.

Having discussion around harm elimination is a medium to bring out those insights. The only precursor is that team discussions need to be fear-free – i.e. staff will not be harmed or perceive a threat of harm for giving constructive feedback and discussion.

10. A more Insightful way of relating to customers, colleagues and the community

Neuroscience is codifying what great marketers, salesmen, negotiators and inspirational leaders have always known. Building trust, loyalty and followship is not about functions, features and benefits. It is not always quantifiable.

A common ingredient is that, in addition to all the rational material, there is a conscious effort to make people feel safe – free from the threat of harm. Whether the tools are non-verbal or storytelling, there is a direct appeal to the non-logical primitive part of our brain where fear, tribal belonging, trust, leadership and followship reside. Difference and otherness are diminished.

Freedom from the threat of harm is at the heart of building a trusted, robust corporation.

Not all corporate actions are benign. Staff are fired, competitors are defeated, natural resources are depleted. How these harmful actions are judged is addressed later.

9.2 Commercial value

Creating a culture of doing no harm has quantifiable benefits, over and above the change in tone, spirit and culture of the corporation. An organisation that has truly embedded the belief that staff can operate free of harm will have:

- A decrease in avoidable incidents because the feedback system for identifying and communicating harmful actions is more effective;
- An increase in resilience because of devolved understanding;
- An increase in staff engagement, which has been proven to improve performance and reduce costs;
- Lower training costs for ethics because staff 'just get it'. Harm is an easily grasped universal. It is an idea that resonates in the same way 'gut feel' operates.

9.3 Harm and corporate social responsibility

Corporate Social Responsibility (CSR) requires an organisation to examine its impact on society – both internally in how it treats its staff and externally in every facet of the environment in which it works. CSR, like values programmes, generates considerable debate about the role of the corporation in society. The

CSR linguistics are complex, relying on duties and obligations, rooted in values that are easy to parse and dismiss.

CSR at its most simple has two actions types: a negative requirement to do no damage and a positive injunction to do good – to act sustainably. The spectrum of the meanings and scope of CSR is vast with high degrees of variance and granularity.

Translating the CSR objectives into the harm language reduces the complexity and increases understanding of the relationship between action and consequence. There is no difference in the CSR harm language from that used in the corporate values. The objectives of CSR are laudable – protect the environment, respect the local society, protect your workers. Expressing these in the language of harm makes everything simpler:

- Do not harm the environment.
- Do not harm the local community.
- Do not harm your employees.

The advent of labour laws and the objective of unions was to protect workers from the harms inflicted by owners. Owners argued that they acted legally but nevertheless inflicted harm on their workers through poor physical conditions, dangerous equipment, non-liveable wages, child labour and health-damaging hours of work. We can all conjure images of eighteenth-century satanic mills and unsafe coal mines. Workers were expendable and replaceable if injured or killed directly, or they fell ill because of unsafe working conditions.

Where the five core Harm Principles and CSR diverge is on the CSR obligation to do good. Doing good is not a primary Harm Principle, however desirable it may appear. However, for corporations wanting to rebuild trust, actively doing good is compelling. Corporations want customers and the broader community to believe they are trustworthy. Making people feel safe by not doing harm is the minimum. Actively remediating harm not of their own making is at another level of corporate trust building, and trust is the foundation of long-term sustainable profitability.

Not doing harm and doing good both reduce fear of being harmed and remove existing harms. Typical harm-reduction activities that are commonly found in the CSR literature include:

- Respecting (not damaging) local culture;
- Proper procedure and fair compensation for acquisition/appropriation of land;
- Environmental protection;
- Worker conditions;
- Enhancing security.

The elimination of a negative is good, but the simple absence of a negative will not promote sustainability. Not doing harm does not move a society

152   *Harm and the corporation*

forward, though it can create a more positive environment to support development. Doing good requires actions that are not just about the present, but also set up conditions for the future reduction of harm. Actions that fall into this category include:

- Local employment including inculcation of the Harm Principles;
- Education – school, technical and employable skills;
- Health education and services;
- Clean water supply;
- Environmental rehabilitation;
- Communications;
- Transport for access to market.

The sceptical public has dismissed many CSR activities and corporate claims, especially in the environment, as green wash or CSR wash. But society is changing, driven by enhanced communications through formal and social media. Expectations are evolving, and the visibility of corporate actions has never been so clear. Corporations are driven by profit and growth. The connection between not doing harm, doing good and profitability is becoming more and more tangible through corporate recognition of the need to build and maintain trust.

Not doing harm and actively reducing harms not of their own making are:

- Measures for CSR;
- A lens for CSR;
- A way of integrating CSR into the everyday business as usual;
- Seen as a logical extension of the way the corporation operates and not seen as a 'green wash' bolt on;
- A rationale for CSR activities that are understandable by all parties.

10 The harms inherent in business

> **Key points:**
>
> - Avoiding harm aligns with good governance, risk management practices and regulatory requirements.
> - Avoiding legal but harmful actions may reduce short-term profits, but eliminates long-term costs of restitution and fines.
> - The Harm Principles do not conflict with making a profit, growth, market economics and competitive practices.
> - Incorporating harm into the Balance Score Card approach shapes behaviour.

'Where is the harm?' is a question asked by staff trying to understand why local custom and practices are not permitted by a centrally imposed policy. Some point out the harms that flow from the very competitive nature of business and the goals of increasing sales and maximising profit. How can these competing forces be reconciled with the constraining dictum to Do No Harm?

10.1 Harm-free practices

The Harm Principles do not preclude making a profit. Nor do they conflict with:

- Corporate values;
- Corporate social responsibility;
- Regulatory requirements;
- Good governance practices;
- Risk management;
- Compliance;
- Community expectations.

154 *Harm and the corporation*

On the contrary, the applied Harm Principles actively improve:

- Understanding of the customer;
- Understanding of the corporation's values programmes;
- An underlying culture of compliance;
- Team interaction;
- Cross-silo interaction;
- Corporate culture;
- Morale and engagement;
- Staff understanding of customer needs, wants and fears;
- Understanding that there is a limit to what can be done in the pursuit of profit, sales and growth.

The Harm Principles are deeply embedded in commercial law governing:

- Consumer protection;
- Financial disclosure;
- Competition, monopolies and predatory behaviour;
- Health and safety;
- Product safety standards;
- Misleading and deceptive conduct.

The Harm Principles do not conflict with doctrines such as voluntary assumption of risk, the enforceability of agreements made between competent parties, and the enforcement of contractual obligations.

Retrenching staff is a necessary activity in most organisations. Laws and rules have been created to minimise the harm to individuals. Done badly, retrenchment, or the fear of retrenchment, is one of the most trust-destroying actions. Staff know it is a possibility, but the criteria for selection, the process, the addressing of individual concerns and emotions and the preservation of individual sense of self-worth need to be addressed, not just for those being retrenched, but for those who remain.

10.2 Harm and commercial practices

Competition is a proven model, yielding innovation, invention, growth and wealth. Yet competition implies winners and losers. Are losers harmed and do they therefore merit protection?

Competition and winning generates growth and the agglomeration of power, to the point where the competition is one-sided. Should power be limited to stop potential harm to both the competitive process and competitors, with ultimate detriment to consumers and the community?

When there is an imbalance of knowledge and power between parties to an agreement, should the weaker be prevented from being harmed by the abuse of power?

The application of the Darwinian survival of the fittest theory to the commercial world has been used to justify 'total business' and deregulation. Darwinism is an amoral, totally selfish model that has at its core the survival and proliferation of DNA at the expense of all other organisms. It explains the role of survival-enabling traits, some of which were covered in Part I: fear, belonging, trusting, leadership and followship. There was no moral value or judgement placed on them. They are simply forces that shape human behaviour, which, when left unchecked, ensure the survival of the most powerful at the expense of the weaker.

Survival is not an ethical mantra. It is an individual genetic behavioural driver that needs to be held in check if social order is to be maintained, which is why societies have developed and enforced norms, codes and laws, often wrapped in complex, self-entrenching language. In most cases, these systems of checks and balances ensure the survival of the society, not just the individual. The Harm Principles and the language of harm are merely ways of expressing these controlling forces in a simpler, unbiased, universally applicable form.

The Harm Principles are politically agnostic. They are neither free-market nor social economy. They are neutral. They provide a yardstick for measurement of the effect of different approaches. This applies to assessing business practices. The Harm Principles provide a way of assessing the impact of the exercise of power of businesses in all dimensions – customers, staff, the community, competitors, suppliers and the Common.

There is a plethora of case law and regulation which limits the harmful exercise of power. Whether this takes the form of competition legislation or striking down usurious penalties, legislators, regulators and courts implicitly look at the underlying harm and where possible prevent it, or rectify and remedy the harm if prevention failed.

The Harm Principles are fully aligned. Nothing in the principles limits charging of fees, enforcing contractual rights and out-competing others in the field, even where the one contracting party may end up in financial difficulty – or feel harmed.

What the Harm Principles provide is an informed and questioning mindset that encourages staff to examine the consequential harm their actions may be setting in train.

It is impossible, and not particularly helpful, to enumerate the types of corporate behaviours that could be harmful. There are all the trust-destroying behaviours summarised in Chapter 3. There are also the obvious actions such as stealing, corrupting, misrepresenting, selling dangerous and defective goods, polluting ... The list is endless, which is why it is more fruitful for corporations to simply internalise the Harm Principles and then apply them at every decision point before actions are taken.

10.3 Profit and target – the 'prime directive'

The single most powerful corporate motivator is the pursuit of profit and target to generate reward and bonuses. Every corporate scandal can be traced to decisions

156 *Harm and the corporation*

taken to ignore, or cover up, harmful behaviours which would interfere with achieving short-term goals.

A few examples illustrate the point:

- Sub-prime mortgages: Financial products were sold to people who could not afford them, creating short-term sales growth and bonus targets;
- The CDO packaged sub-prime mortgages into saleable products;
- Faking emission standards by VW to gain competitive advantage and sales by claiming their cars were greener, more efficient and more powerful than competitors;
- Misleading and deceptive sales practices;
- Wells Fargo: Creating unauthorised accounts;
- Barings, UBS ... Turning a blind-eye to extraordinary profits made by 'rogue traders' which secured bonuses for the team and senior executives.

10.4 Distortions from the pressure to succeed

> Success is the ability to go from one failure to another with no loss of enthusiasm.
>
> (Anon.)

Most civilisations have glorified success, whether on the battlefield, in business or amorous conquests. We are defined more by what we achieve and have achieved than by how well we behave. From childhood, we are encouraged to do well in examinations and sport. Winning is good; failing is bad. Success is important, but the drive to be successful can distort the person and the organisation. We have all seen the dark side: cheating in exams, doping in sport, mis-selling financial products, lying in corporate accounts.

Huge bonuses drove dealers and product creators to engineer the 2008 financial meltdown. Those outside watched in awe as fortunes doubled and tripled and rode the wave of optimism, too often abandoning traditional financial caution for the new certainty, borrowing against the rising capital value of our homes. We flipped, twisted and rode the markets up, trumpeting our success with new toys.

The blame for meltdown is not just for those at the centre who created and peddled the financial euphoria, or the regulators and their political masters who basked in the reflected sunlight, but also those in the broader society who fuelled their addiction for 'betting on a sure thing' so we could get 'something for nothing'.

The cause of the meltdown does not rest solely on the head of Mr and Mrs Everyperson but also on a society where share price and corporate success, measured impossibly in quarters, drives and distorts corporate behaviour. The pressure on the Chairman and CEO flows down to every nook and cranny of the organisation.

Cost savings to support profit often denude the organisation of the capacity to manage the dark side – the risk of poor and non-compliant behaviour. The focus is on the bottom line, not the dark alley that does not appear on the balance sheet. The short termers lose sight of the greatest invisible asset on the balance sheet – trust.

Resources are too often focussed on the short-term productive, to the detriment of short-term effectiveness and long-term sustainability.

The harm principles in practice

In a workshop with call centre staff, they initially believed they had no power to inflict harm, but without prompting or guidance they quickly came to appreciate the inherent potential harms in their role as the primary communication touch point for customers.

They deeply understood why having clear, honest and open communications would be good for the customer and the harm that could be done if communication was opaque or misleading. This may seem trivial, but the impact on morale, in an already low-morale role, was significant. Following the workshop, the number of customer complaints about the call centre declined. Staff engagement increased and staff turnover declined.

Changes to scripts and protocols were implemented with a harm minimisation focus. Staff felt better about themselves and their roles. Some high-pressure, target-driven managers felt it would decrease sales. Total sales value did not decline, but the product mix did change. Customers were more likely to get what they needed, not what the local product manager wanted pushed.

A workshop at higher organisational levels identified poor sales practices, which ultimately became the subject of regulatory intervention and massive fines. The house cleaning post-workshops and pre-regulatory intervention greatly reduced the multi-million dollar fines the experts said would be levied.

Harmful, silo-entrenching behaviours were commonly identified and plans were put in place to rectify them. Harms identified in 'them and us' mindsets helped improve communication and collaboration.

What is exciting and powerful is that staff collectively identified the harms, the harmful behaviours, the emotional and financial costs, and believed that change was possible and practical.

The Harm Principles blunt the unthinking pursuit of profit. Maximising profit with indifference to the harm generated is a short-term strategy that will ultimately destroy corporate trustworthiness, and trust is one of the most valuable corporate assets.

10.5 Balancing harm and risk

As a species, it appears that we are programmed to take risks. It is part of the evolutionary process. We try, we fail and so avoid in the future. We try and succeed and so repeat the successful activity. We took risks as cavemen stalking the woolly mammoth. Traditional tribal rites of passage often encompassed mastering risk and danger.

Every risk involves a potential harm. Taking risks with your own person and property is different to putting other people at risk of harm. The very nature of

158 *Harm and the corporation*

incorporation and the artifice of the corporate veil has insulated boards, executives and staff from the risks they engage in on behalf of the corporation.

Incorporation has disconnected our primal urge for risk taking from the primal fear of personal consequence. Freedom from consequence, coupled with the bonus-profit-growth prime directive unleashed predictable behaviours and consequences.

Making employees aware of the Harm Principles, and giving them an understanding of how their actions can harm, reduces ambiguity and opacity. Adding the harm heuristic simplifies, so aiding thinking, understanding and decision making. It allows employees to align their personal value to not be harmed to the meaning of the corporate values, and how these values should be applied in their individual roles.

When the entire organisation is harm aware, fear of harm for speaking out is removed and organisational resilience is increased. It becomes harder for individual proximate managers to drive harmful behaviour, including taking on unauthorised risk.

10.6 Harm in the balanced score card

> When I was younger I thought success was something different. I thought: 'When I grow up, I want to be famous. I want to be a star. I want to be in movies. When I grow up I want to see the world, drive nice cars. I want to have groupies.' But my idea of success is different today. For me, the most important thing in your life is to live your life with integrity and not to give into peer pressure, to try to be something that you're not. To live your life as an honest and compassionate person. To contribute in some way.
>
> (Ellen DeGeneres, Tulane Commencement Speech, 2009)

The balanced score card is used to align actions of staff with the objectives of the organisation with the objective of improving overall importance. Balanced score cards, as the name implies, introduced into performance assessment several factors in addition to the traditional financial and sales goals. The elements that comprise a score card are flexible to suit the strategy and needs of an organisation at a point in time.

Managers have been assessed, for example, on how they have implemented equal opportunity policies, IT systems, communications and, of course, financial metrics. The value of the formalised balanced score card is that recognition and reward are tied to a broader spectrum of factors. It operates on the assumption that people are rational and will attempt to maximise their remuneration and prospects. Thus, if the assessment is only on sales, then the focus will be on sales. Other operational issues will not get attention and when they conflict with the sales target, they will be ignored.

> What gets measured gets done.

The balanced score card provides an opportunity for the board to shape behaviour by including in the score card an assessment for adherence to behavioural outcomes. Harm management is a simple way of addressing the behavioural assessment.

The weighting given to the behavioural component will indicate the importance that the board places on the desired behaviour. Imagine a hypothetical score card with four elements, of which one was behaviour. With equal weighting, behaviour has a 25 per cent impact on reward and ranking. The weighting could be redistributed, with financial performance at 70 per cent and the remaining three at 10 per cent each. The second sends a clear message. Behaviour does not matter.

> Show me the money!
>
> (*Jerry Maguire*, Tristar Pictures, 1996)

The score card principle is simple; the way it is implemented is not. It is often complex and counterproductive.

An innovative approach is to remove behaviour from the matrix formula and instead use it as a multiplier of the total bonus. In the formula here the amount of bonus received is base bonus multiplied by the sum of the components of the score card (F1 to Fn) multiplied by the Behaviour Index (BI), where the BI has a range from 0 to 2. A behaviour score of 2 would double the bonus. A score of 0 would eliminate it.

Bonus = \$base x (F1% + F2% + F3%) x BI

This type of remuneration model puts all the bonus at risk and because the BI is visible and discrete, easily reportable for follow-up action. The elegance of this model is that upside bonuses are not limited by the model and in fact can be doubled.

> Half of the harm that is done in this world is due to people who want to feel important. They don't mean to do harm but the harm does not interest them.
>
> (TS Elliot)

If harm was included in the Behavioural Index (or as a significant element of the traditional balanced score card), then people would become very interested in the harm they inflict.

10.7 Enabling third-party harm

'Don't be evil', in the Google manifesto, implies a range of undefined moral judgements. What does 'evil' mean? Is it the actions of the Cold War spy? The actions of liberation armies? The behaviour of master criminals? The actions of child pornographers? The writings of dissident poets? The setting up of a school for girls that offends the leaders in a deeply religious community? The security agencies collecting email and telephone records?

Evil is contextual, depending on location and time in history. What is evil today may not be tomorrow. An evil action in place A may be fine across the border in place B.

160 *Harm and the corporation*

Perhaps the implicit agenda in the Google motto is that evil equates to 'un-American', which itself is ambiguous because America is, in the eyes of some, 'the great Satan!' In the Google IPO letter the intent is clarified to align with the 6th Harm Principle.

> Don't be evil. We believe strongly that in the long term, we will be better served-as shareholders and in all other ways-by a company that does good things for the world even if we forgo some short term gains.

It would be more accurate and have greater impact if Google tied itself to a standard – *do no harm.*

10.8 Why behaviour change programmes fail

Untold millions have been wasted on marginally effective ethics and values training. The lack of impact and resonance is not because the presenters are boring or the compliance and ethics officers are not diligent. On the contrary, presenters can be clear, witty and engaging and still have no impact on future behaviour. They can make you think, but after the course is over, the enthusiasm wanes and business as usual returns.

The training is like stirring a bucket of water with your hand. While you are providing the energy and motive force, the water will swirl and some may even be spilled. As soon as your hand is removed, the momentum slows, till eventually the water is still, as if nothing had ever happened. All that is left is a wet hand, some spilled water and a tick in the box – training delivered.

The purpose of values and ethics programmes is to change behaviour, not to get a tick in the box. The question for leaders is: 'Why does our massive investment have such small dividends?'

The usual excuses, which are all valid, include:

- Lack of commitment from the top;
- Poor tone from the top. The senior executives are not role-models for the desired behaviours;
- Lack of resources. Insufficient budget to be get real coverage and visibility;
- Lip service – do as I say, not as I do.

These contribute to a programme's failure, but even assuming 100 per cent commitment and support from the leadership team and sufficient funding, behaviour change programmes fail when they are based on:

- Traditional ethical language of right and wrong, good and bad, implicitly ignoring local cultural norms and practices;
- Top down messaging as the sole source of wisdom and truth. When there is no programme to ensure active engagement by the local managers, the message is vulnerable to local distortion;

The harms inherent in business   161

- A one-size-fits-all message. This is impersonal. The usual communication tools such as mass emails, podcasts, screen savers, posters and even social media, even 'live' broadcasts, have limited potential to connect with the individual in a way so that afterwards they can answer the question, *'what's in it for me?'*;
- A big bang campaign without an ongoing programme of reinforcement;
- Content that is rules- and data-based. Prescriptive programmes will create awareness and understanding, but may not necessarily impact attitude and behaviour;
- E-learning which is chosen because it is the easiest and cheapest tool;
- Middle managers are not actively responsible.

And there are more fundamental reasons for failure.

1. The messages of the programme generate conflict with growth and profit drivers.
2. Performance in the organisation is judged by competing, often informal, values, not those promoted in the course.
3. Performance appraisal and reward systems do not have sufficient emphasis on the 'how'.
4. The way the material is presented, does not resonate. 'I get what was said, but what does that mean for me in the work I do? What's in it for me? Why should I care?' This approach is counterproductive because it fails to address the human condition – why we trust, follow and believe something is right, or wrong, and then act on it.

10.9 Address how we change beliefs and attitude

To understand behaviour change it is necessary to first grasp how attitudes, opinions and beliefs are formed and changed. Unfortunately, for our data- and rule-focused corporate world, research has established that the presentation of irrefutable truth and facts has limited effect on changing opinions.

The underlying flaw in corporate behaviour-change programmes is the over-reliance on the belief that knowledge drives behaviour. Knowledge is important, but not sufficient. People smoke, drink, eat the wrong foods, eat too much and have unsafe sex. We know the rules of the road, yet we speed. We deliberately put ourselves at risk and break rules, especially if we think we can get away with it.

How many parents could claim that simply educating their child about what was right and wrong was sufficient to achieve compliance? Once the threshold of cognition is traversed, kids still don't listen. They know, they understand and they ignore.

Research in neuroscience is revealing why facts do not change attitudes and beliefs. Yet the primary tool used by corporations to achieve compliant behaviour is content-rich training for ethics and a multitude of policies and codes. If knowledge does not shape behaviour in the natural world, why do corporations persist in the

162 *Harm and the corporation*

belief that the act of simply stepping through the corporate portal imbues knowledge with mystical powers to shape employee behaviour?

For the most part, our natural world is ordered. Most people follow most of the rules most of the time. They even obey laws they have never heard of: blissful, ignorant, compliant.

The true controlling forces are social. Most laws in stable societies reflect social norms. Our behaviour is normalised by our family, our friends, our peers and our perceptions of the world. We are socialised. Positive reinforcement and approval are paired with consequence for non-compliance. Consequences have a vast dynamic range from rebuke to shunning, physical harm and imprisonment.

Our final models may or may not align with what we were formally taught by our parents, at school or in our religious instruction, or even in the statutes. The developmental process is complex. We ultimately learn to calibrate right and wrong according to our personal scale that evolved with maturity, experience and knowledge.

When we enter a new society, whether we adhere to the social rules or not, we will be influenced by the degree to which the rules align with our internal values and the risks and immediacy of consequence for non-compliance. How we ultimately behave is not always logical to the outside observer. It is therefore not predictable, because much of our decision making will involve the unconscious application of internalised heuristics to judge what to do in unfamiliar circumstances.

Entering the corporate portal does not change how we learn and develop. It does not change our biology or our inherited instincts and drivers, yet corporate norm formation is built primarily on four logical, knowledge-based processes:

- Values and rules are developed and published.
- Employees are educated on the content and meaning of the values and rules.
- Compliance with the values and rules is monitored.
- There are consequences for non-compliance.

Less effort is spent on designing, nurturing and deliberately shaping the corporate culture to achieve the desired behaviours. It is one thing to have an idea; it is another to have the idea acted on. This raises two questions:

1. 'How do ideas become part of the collective and individual consciousness?' and
2. Once the idea is understood, 'what triggers action?'

Ideas become part of our consciousness through formal instruction and social interaction – friends, family and community. It can also be a random process, like Brownian motion, where there is a random collision between a person and an idea. But Brownian motion is allied to the process of entropy where the energy injected dissipates – like tea getting cold in a cup – into the atmosphere.

For an idea to take hold, like the idea of democracy in the Arab Spring, there need to be powerful forces at play. For an idea to make a difference, it needs an atomic reaction, where the total energy released continues to increase as the matter is transformed. Atomic reactions require not only the reactive material but also powerful environmental forces and a triggering event.

The same is true in business systems and society at large. In business, the initiating power comes from the board and senior management. The decision to change requires a triggering event – whether in the mind of a leader or in the environment in which the corporation operates.

There are also actions that are reactive, such as boards effecting change to comply, often reluctantly, with changes in the law and regulatory environment. Whether the stimulus is a desire to do good or to stay compliant is irrelevant, so long as the board is truly committed to the new behaviours.

Using the language of harm is also important because most[1] laws and regulations are implemented to prevent harm. Policies and procedures are the corporate response to the harm prevention required by the laws and regulations. Unfortunately, the nexus between the policies and procedures and the harms they are intended to prevent is often lost in the mind-numbing, prescriptive behavioural language. Identifying the harms being addressed by policies and procedures makes it easier for staff to understand why the policies and procedures are important. Using the language of harms instead of right and wrong or illegal ensures meaning flows across all cultures and local practices.

10.10 The impact of harm on mindset

A harm-aware corporation requires every staff member at every level to consider a number of key questions.

- What is it that I do that could cause harm to:

  - My team;
  - My colleagues;
  - My company;
  - My customer;
  - My community.

- In the action/decision I am about to take, who could be harmed:

  - Now;
  - In the future (latent harm).

10.11 Legal but harmful

The model

Feedback from tens of thousands of workshop attendees has reinforced the value of one discussion point – identifying actions that may be permitted in law, but which may generate harm.

The concept is illustrated by a simple set of Venn diagrams (see Figure 10.1).

164 *Harm and the corporation*

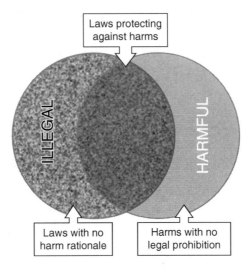

Figure 10.1 The interstion of harm and legality

- The circle on the left represents everything that is illegal. Everything inside the circle is forbidden by law. By definition, everything outside the circle on the left is not illegal. There are no laws prohibiting the activity.
- The circle on the right represents everything that is harmful, within the definition of harm used in this book. Everything outside the circle is implicitly not harmful.
- Where the circles overlap illustrates that there are laws which make harmful actions illegal.
- However, as you can see, there are laws in the left circle that are outside the harm circles. These laws are not designed to prevent harm. They include laws about tastes, beliefs and controls to make society function.
- The last segment on the right represents harmful actions that are not illegal.

It is this final segment that is crucial to shaping future behaviour. Too often, executives have exhorted their lawyers to find gaps in the law and then required staff to act. It is only when the harm results in public outcry that the behaviour stops and the law changes.

The gap mindset has driven behaviours in the finance industry to redefine behaviours as legal, which has resulted in hundreds of billions in fines, still to be paid by global banks. The damage has been done and the bonuses paid.

How does it work?

Workshop attendees are asked several carefully structured questions presented in a specific order:

The harms inherent in business 165

1. What kinds of harm are there? (Examples: physical, financial, emotional).
2. What differences are there in the impact of these harms based on differences in race, religion, sex, nationality, age ... ? (Answer: none).
3. What makes an action illegal? (Answer: There is a law against it).
4. What harms can we inflict on ourselves that are legal? (Examples: smoking, drinking, overeating).
5. In our area of work, what harms have been made illegal? (Examples: fraud, theft, polluting, mis-selling, labour laws. The potential list is enormous).

The final question is at the heart of the programme:

6. What actions are not illegal, but may cause harm to our external customers? (Examples: confusing sales material, selling to those who do not need it, exploiting gaps in the law).

    Trophy hunters have a bad habit of conflating the legal and the moral ('I hunt. It's legal. Get over it.') read T-shirts American college student Kendall Jones printed up after she was criticized for killing an African lion.[2]

If the Harm Principles had been common currency, then the selling of financial products to those who could not afford them, or did not need them, would have been questioned. The Harm Principles would have impeded, or at least slowed, the primal driver that we don't care about individual default because we can bundle them together, wrap an insurance protection around them and we will be making money.

If one assumes that what was done was legal, the actions were still harmful.

Awareness is only the first step. The detailed implementation programme is being codified and will be published in *How?* A step by step guide for control staff, HR, communications and training.

10.12 Integrate harm into the decision matrices

Integrating the assessment of harm into every action/decision point reaches into every corner and every activity. It will influence the questions asked of potential employees, suppliers and venture partners. Every step of the product life cycle can simply, without great cost or delay, consider harm in supply, manufacture, distribution, marketing, sales and disposal. The potential harm could be reported in the same way as costs and profitability, instead of, as is common, buried in multiple risk assessments.

Harm analysis is not a substitute for risk analysis, but rather the manifestation of harm is a risk to be consciously managed. Whether harm is included as a formal line item in risk and compliance assessments is less important than having conscious thought and discussion about potential harms become part of the invisible processes that happen automatically. Harm identification and remediation need to be built into the culture, not bolted on as a system or process.

166 *Harm and the corporation*

While the foregoing established the value of harm as an approach, it is in the end only an idea. To be truly valuable harm will need to be integrated into our decision models – individual, corporate and public. It is not possible to simply replace seven billion mindsets developed over centuries.

What is both possible and necessary is to begin the dialogue and introduce the idea of considering harm as a conscious process, even if ultimately the decision is to ignore the harm and risk, inflicting the harm regardless of consequences, particularly for the long term. This outcome is based on a not atypical decision model, driven by expediency and targets.

10.13 Conclusion

The Harm Principles provide a unifying language that transcends cultural and contextual differences and allows a single set of values to be globally relevant. A corporate culture which has *legal but harmful* embedded in its psyche will need less compliance controls.

Changing the culture, the way an organisation feels, believes and acts, is far cheaper than a rules-based enforcement model, yielding greater positive actions and fewer negative reactions. The more positive the culture, the less rules are required and the less needs to be spent on compliance and enforcement.

In the perfect world, the *legal but harmful* mindset becomes a virtuous circle, nurturing employee engagement, customer and market trust and, consequentially, profitability.

Regardless of industry, location or size, being trustworthy must be a central plank of every organisation's culture. Adopting the Harm Principles is a simple way to build a solid trustworthy foundation for corporate behaviour.

The Harm Principles also provide a self-governing mechanism that, while promoting adherence to a single value suite, limits the formation of masks and the distortions that flow from extreme adherence to a set of values.

The goal for corporations is simple:

> Harm awareness and thinking becomes part of the invisible culture and helps define 'the way we do things round here.'

Notes

1 There are many laws and regulations that are procedural, and, unfortunately, some poor laws which do not address harm mitigation at all, but enshrine the values of the legislature.
2 *The Independent,* 3 July 2014.

Index

Aborigine 17, 40
alpha 14, 120–1, 130, 133, 144
altruism 3, 12, 55, 96–8, 126
Aristotle 37, 54

Behaviour Index 159
beliefs 1, 8, 9, 12, 19–54, 58, 62, 66, 71–2,
   79, 81, 84, 87, 89–95, 98, 111, 119,
   135–7, 161, 164
belonging 3, 5–7, 13–15, 41–3, 96, 101,
   119–120, 123–124, 126, 143, 150, 155
bribery 48, 119, 130
build trust 8–11, 54–5, 60–4, 66, 72, 84,
   147, 149, 150–1

case studies 19–20, 22, 139
changing beliefs 20–2, 25, 98, 161
compliance, legal and corporate ix, 1, 11,
   20, 28, 47, 52–4, 73, 83, 110, 118, 122,
   128, 140–3, 146, 153–4, 160–2, 165–6;
   social and norm i, 20, 39
controls 26, 30, 33, 43–4, 53, 79, 91–2, 104,
   117, 135, 164, 166
corporate drivers of behaviour 109–125;
   corporate veil 114; distance 116; dual
   worlds 124–5; globalisation, impact of on
   117–19; human nature 119; layers of clay
   120–21; leadership and followship 120;
   legal framework 111–12; ownership and
   control 113; scale and structure 115–117;
   survival 123; tribalism 124
corporate social responsibility 55, 96, 146,
   150–3
corporate values ix, xi–xii, 35, 39–40, 64–5,
   67, 111, 124–134, 137, 147, 151, 153, 158
CSR *see* corporate social responsibility
culture i–x, 11, 16–18, 26, 30, 32, 36–7, 44,
   48, 57, 64–5, 73, 76, 79, 81, 83, 94, 96,
   99, 111, 113–120, 122, 128, 130–1,
   134–154, 162–3, 166

dark side 138, 156
Darwin, C. 22, 29, 90, 96, 123, 155
dehumanise 13, 30, 86, 92, 94, 103
demonise 30–1, 42, 65, 92, 133
destroying trust ix, 55, 56, 58, 60–3, 74, 155
distrust 3–5, 7–8, 10, 32, 56–58, 67,
   119–20, 124
DNA 3–22, 31, 55, 60 78, 96, 101, 123, 155
dysfunction indicators 135–6, 140; growth
   imperative 141; leadership behaviours
   141, 145

Edison, T. 30
egalitarian 14, 37
emotion 4, 6, 8, 13–14, 47; alignment and
   engagement 143, 145–7; altruism 97–8;
   emotional harm 74–5, 81, 89, 91–2; threat
   of harm 101, 124
engagement ix, xi, 32, 55, 57, 99, 115, 122,
   124, 129–130, 135, 137, 143–6, 149–50,
   154, 157, 160, 166
ENRON 129, 131–2, 136, 140
ethics xii, 3, 11, 22–56, 71–72, 110, 119,
   126–7, 134, 146, 148, 150, 160–1

facts viii–ix, 3, 7, 9, 14, 17–22, 25–30, 34,
   39, 42, 53, 55–7, 59, 66, 89–90, 92, 98,
   105, 110, 148, 161
faith xi, 8–9, 24–28, 30, 42, 45–46, 52, 56,
   58–62, 78–80, 87–97, 110, 119
fear xi, 3–13, 16, 22, 24, 26, 30, 41, 43, 53,
   55–59, 63–65, 78, 91–2, 101, 104–5, 110,
   114, 124, 126, 133, 135–8, 140–3, 146–7,
   149–51, 154–5, 158

168   *Index*

find the gap 51, 52, 83, 100,
  127, 143
following orders 34, 120, 123, 140, 149
followship 9, 42, 115, 119–20, 126, 128–9,
  139–40, 150, 155

globalisation i, 4, 11, 37, 46, 50–1, 78,
  105, 117
Google IPO manifesto 147, 159–60

Haidt, J. 11–13, 22
Harari, Y. 16, 22, 124
harm exclusions 99; facts 89; construct not
  the person 92; myths, beliefs, religions 90
harm: decision matrices xi, 165; risk
  management 140, 153
Harm Principle 1. do no harm 82
Harm Principle 2. freedom from harm 83
Harm Principle 3. harming in self-defence 84
Harm Principle 4. proportional harming 85
Harm Principle 5. balance of harms 85
Harm Principle 6. reduce harms 95–6, 98–9
Harm Principles i, x–xii, 25, 54, 56, 64–5,
  71–105, 126, 146, 151–8, 165–6;
  simplicity of xiii, 72, 74–5, 77, 82–3
harms, physical 73–5, 162
harms, psychological 65, 71, 73–5, 80–1,
  85–6, 89, 93, 94
harms to the Common 71, 73–7, 80, 83–4,
  87, 89, 91, 101, 155
harm, incitement to 77–8, 92
harm and institutionalised punishment 39,
  45, 71, 74, 80, 85, 91, 93–4, 101, 103;
  threat of harm 101
harm and laws: examples of legalised
  harming 48–51; sexual preference 49;
  prostitution 49; slave ownership 49;
  changing legality and bad laws 45
harm, nature of 72, 73, 76, 148
harm, persistence of 75, 80
harm, quantum of 74–5, 78, 80, 85–6, 89,
  101, 110, 117
harm, righteous infliction of xi, 31, 40, 45,
  71, 86, 91–4, 139–40
harm and religion 71–6, 78–81, 84, 89–95,
  98–9, 102–4, 165
harm and the state 45–7, 74, 76, 87
harm, susceptibility to 81
harm, universality of i, x, 54, 71–3, 76–7,
  80–3, 89, 155
harms to property 71, 73–6, 80, 83–4, 86,
  87–9, 91, 93, 100, 101, 103–4, 157
Hippocrates i, 13, 82

Jekyll and Hyde syndrome 140, 145
Jobs, S. 17, 19, 22, 62–3, 65, 122, 124,
  135–7, 143, 145

Kant, E. 37

layers of clay 109, 121–2
leaders and leadership i, 3, 7, 9–11,
  13–4, 16–17, 21–4, 33–4, 40,
  42–3, 53, 56, 59, 64–7, 78, 84, 95, 97,
  101–2, 109–10, 115–26, 128–9 131,
  134–138, 141, 143–47, 150, 155,
  159–160, 163
legal but harmful 146–7, 153, 163, 166
libertarian xi, 37, 88, 98
logic in behaviour viii–xi, 3–35, 41–2, 45,
  46, 65–6, 71, 86, 88, 92, 95, 99, 105, 110,
  120, 124, 162

market, effect on: behaviour i, 11, 15, 17,
  31–2, 42, 53–4, 57–8, 61–5, 75, 78, 96,
  109, 111–3, 118–9, 123, 130–4, 138, 141,
  166; and harm 153
Mill, J. 37
Mindset xi, 4, 53, 83, 95, 105, 111, 118, 141,
  142, 149, 155, 157, 163–4, 16
morals, morality and harms i, ix–x, xii,
  3–22, 24, 28, 29, 31, 35–38, 40, 43, 50,
  52–3, 57, 72–3, 76–7, 86–9, 92, 94, 103,
  132, 147, 155, 165
morality mask: concept 40, 43, 132–134,
  138–143; market morality mask 132
myth ix, 13–17, 31, 40, 42, 53, 88–90, 98,
  102, 112, 131–9, 148

neuroscience i, vii, 10–11, 21, 24, 41, 96,
  150, 161

oxytocin 10–12

philosophy x, 25, 36–7, 72–3, 87, 89, 99,
  103, 113
Plato 38, 45, 54
policies ix–x, 19, 22, 25, 32–3, 43–4,
  110, 118–9, 127–8, 134–5, 158,
  161, 163
procedures *see* policies

regulation and regulators: intervention ix,
  xi, xii, 32, 35, 41, 44, 47–54, 57, 61,
  63–5, 67, 110–11, 117–19, 127–33, 153,
  155–7, 163; regulatory dilemma 102–3

Index 169

religion i, x–xii, 7, 11, 14, 16, 18, 23–34, 36, 38–9, 42, 50, 54, 65; harm and 71–6, 78–81, 84, 89–95, 98–9, 102–4, 165

safe and safety 4, 6–7, 11–12, 15, 21–22, 47, 53, 56, 59–60, 63–6, 77, 84, 92, 98, 101–5, 115–18, 123, 126, 145, 150–1, 154, 161

Sapiens 16, 22, 124

Schein, E. 57, 136

social attitude to harming 103

story: power of 13–20, 22, 34, 43, 98, 135, 137, 150; song-lines 17

survival drivers: innate 3–7, 10, 12–14, 17–18, 22, 24, 31, 42; relationship to trust and harm 56, 62, 66, 72, 78, 84, 96–98; in the corporation 110, 114, 119–124, 136, 144, 155

tribalism: innate 6, 13–15, 30, 41–2, 51, 102, 105; in the corporation 116–17, 124

Trump, D. 60, 65, 92, 117, 133

trust i, ix, xi–xii, 1, 4–5, 7–13, 17, 22, 24, 32–33, 35, 41, 49–50, 53, 59–67, 72–3, 84, 99, 101, 105, 110, 114–15, 117–20, 122, 124, 126, 133, 137–8, 141, 143, 146–7, 149, 151–2, 154–5, 157, 161, 166

utilitarian xi, 14, 37, 88

values ix–xii, 36; corporate 22, 23, 35, 39, 44, 65, 120–5, 126–134, 136–138; impact on laws 46, 50, 51, 54; power of 19, 21, 35, 40–3, 55, 61 see trust; relationship to the Harm Principles 93; religious 29; shared as a basis for trust 9–12, 35

values veil 37, 39–40, 125, 132, 139

Zak, P. 10